GREAT LIVES OBSERVED

MacARTHUR

Edited by
LAWRENCE S. WITTNER

There is no substitute for victory.

—Douglas MacArthur

A SPECTRUM BOOK

PRENTICE-HALL, INC., ENGLEWOOD CLIFFS, N. J.

Dedicated to imprisoned war resisters around the world

LAWRENCE S. WITTNER, *editor of this volume in the Great Lives Observed series, is Assistant Professor of History at Vassar College. He is the author of* Rebels Against War *and of numerous articles on twentieth-century American foreign policy.*

Current printing (last number): 10 9 8 7 6 5 4 3 2 1

C–13-541433-4
P–13-541425-3

Library of Congress Catalog Card Number: 77-160530

Printed in the United States of America

PRENTICE-HALL INTERNATIONAL, INC., (*London*)
PRENTICE-HALL OF AUSTRALIA, PTY. LTD. (*Sydney*)
PRENTICE-HALL OF CANADA, LTD. (*Toronto*)
PRENTICE-HALL OF INDIA PRIVATE LIMITED (*New Delhi*)
PRENTICE-HALL OF JAPAN (*Tokyo*)

Contents

iii

PART TWO
DOUGLAS MACARTHUR VIEWED BY HIS CONTEMPORARIES

v

Introduction

In the summer of 1932, Governor Franklin D. Roosevelt of New York, the Democratic nominee for President of the United States, sat chatting at his Hyde Park estate with Rexford Tugwell, his advisor. They were interrupted by a telephone call from the flamboyant Louisiana Governor, Huey P. Long. After the call, Roosevelt remarked that Long was "one of the two most dangerous men in the country." Tugwell asked him if the second was the popular "radio priest," Father Charles Coughlin. Roosevelt demurred. "Oh no," he stated, "the other is Douglas MacArthur."

What Roosevelt feared about MacArthur was almost exactly what caused uneasiness and sometimes alarm among later generations: his symbolic appeal, in times of crisis, as "the man on horseback." Roosevelt told Tugwell that among some industrialists and men of power in American life, the economic situation of the thirties had generated a disdain for democracy and a desire for strong leadership. In Europe, the dangerous trend toward acceptance of Napoleonic and fascist leaders was all too clear. And of all the potential Caesars in American life, as Tugwell summarized their conversation, "there was none so well endowed with charm, tradition and majestic appearance as MacArthur."

There is no reason, of course, to believe that MacArthur ever planned to seize power through extralegal means. Although he maintained an extraordinary level of political activity for a career officer in the United States Army—including several serious bids for the GOP Presidential nomination—few would contend that he fancied himself as an American dictator. Most critics, like the acerbic Secretary of the Interior, Harold Ickes, simply found him incredibly vain. "MacArthur is the type of man," wrote Ickes in 1933, "who thinks that when he gets to heaven, God will step down from the great white throne and bow him into His vacated seat." Because they trusted MacArthur's commitment to democratic procedures, and because they respected his military capability, Presidents Roosevelt and Truman appointed the general to the highest of offices. Only in 1951 did his actions raise the specter of a military *coup*.

While MacArthur never moved to take control of the government, however, his vast and fervent following was considerably less trust-worthy. Throughout much of his career, they seemed eager to cata-pult him into power. The adulatory letters in his files bear witness to the authoritarian potential beneath the surface of American life: "We love you, almost to the worshipping point." "There is no doubt that you are the Leader we need." "We need somebody *strong* in Washington." "You are BIG enough to do a complete housecleaning of parasitic bureaucrats." "We could do with a military government for a change." "General Douglas MacArthur is indeed a Man of Destiny." MacArthur's military staff, noted for its adoration of the general, did not hold strikingly different views. One letter from a subordinate officer to MacArthur concluded: "In humble reverence we, the members of your staff, pray to almighty God that he bless and preserve the greatest figure in all history." These sentiments, when added to the anti-Semitic, racist, nativist, xenophobic, and blood-thirsty views of his most frenzied supporters, boded ill for the future of representative institutions.

Moreover, MacArthur enjoyed enormous popularity among mil-lions of Americans. In 1944, thanks to his wartime prominence, public opinion surveys named him as one of the three Republicans most fre-quently supported for the presidency. By 1948, the pollsters predicted that the general would be an easy victor over Harry Truman.

Truman's dismissal of MacArthur from his commands in 1951 lifted the general's star to its zenith. Tremendous crowds turned out to greet him. In New York, an estimated 7,500,000 people jammed the sidewalks to cheer his passing car, discarding 16,600,000 pounds of litter in an orgy of delight. Two critics of MacArthur have described the scene as follows:

> New York threw together the biggest, most bedazzling show in its frenetic history. There were streamers on the spires of Trinity Church. Forty thousand union longshoremen struck for the afternoon. . . . School children and office workers were given the afternoon off; even the pajama-clad inmates of psychiatric wards were brought outdoors to watch the spectacle. Eighteen victims of hysteria—none of them from the psychiatric wards—had to be carted away from the demonstration.

Similar throngs greeted MacArthur's triumphal entourage in cities throughout the country.

While the President was booed and burned in effigy by angry crowds, denounced as a drunkard, a son-of-a-bitch and a traitor by the na-tion's political leaders, and marked for impeachment by the Republican party, General MacArthur evoked a great surge of frenzied support. State legislatures lauded his service to the nation and denounced his "political assassination," and Congress invited him to present his views to a joint session of the House and Senate. At the conclusion of his speech, which drew the largest radio and television audience up to that time in history, MacArthur reached the pinnacle of his popular influence. "We heard God speak here today," Missouri Representative Dewey Short cried out, "God in the flesh, the voice of God." Other Congressmen, wiping their moist eyes, agreed that it was the greatest speech ever delivered. Polls revealed that Americans not only strongly opposed the firing of MacArthur, but also that the general would be an easy victor over Truman in the coming Presidential election.

But even this tidal wave of MacArthurite sentiment failed to topple the American government and sweep the general into power. Although MacArthur gave the keynote address at the Republican National Convention in 1952, and received a frantic ovation when his name was placed in nomination, that parley finally nominated a more moderate and less dashing general: Eisenhower.[1] Unlike Charles de Gaulle, whose personality, views, and career to some extent paralleled his own, MacArthur never came to power. Throughout his life he remained no more than a potential "man on horseback"—but what potential!

Douglas MacArthur was born in the Arsenal Barracks of Little Rock, Arkansas in early 1880. The Norfolk, Virginia newspapers, loyal to his mother's family home in that city, declared somewhat confusingly: "Douglas MacArthur was born on January 26, while his parents were away."

Young Douglas was the latest in a long line of military men that, in later years, he enjoyed tracing back to the Scottish Clan Campbell. "There is nothing older, except the hills, MacArtair and the devil," ran an ancient Scottish adage. His father, Arthur MacArthur, was a Union colonel in the Civil War at age nineteen, a captain who relocated Indians in the Southwest, and the military governor of the Philippines who crushed Aguinaldo's insurrection. Arthur MacArthur died in 1912 at his Civil War regiment's fiftieth reunion when, after the recounting of old war stories and the singing of old war songs,

[1] This choice particularly outraged MacArthur supporters at the convention, who consisted almost entirely of "Christian Nationalists," since they unaccountably believed Eisenhower to be Jewish. Eventually, they placed MacArthur's name on the ballot in seven states as part of their "Stop Ike-the-Kike" campaign, but he received less than twenty thousand votes.

he rose to address the gathering, only to collapse of apoplexy partway through his speech. As he lay dying, his former soldiers knelt and recited the Lord's Prayer. The adjutant lay the regimental flag over the body of his fallen commander, and then he, too, collapsed, of a fatal paralytic stroke. As a child, the last words Douglas heard every night were those of his mother, assuring him that he would some day be a great man like his father.

Douglas' attachment to his mother, Mary Pinkney Hardy, was extraordinary. The descendant of generations of southern military men, "Pinky" Hardy married Arthur MacArthur on May 19, 1875, beginning what Douglas recalled as "thirty-seven years of perfect union." Few mothers have been as close to their sons as "Pinky" MacArthur, who lived with Douglas almost continuously until her death in 1935, when he was fifty-five years old. She even accompanied him to West Point, where she resided for four years, superintending his education, receiving daily reports from him on his activities, and sending him little notes of encouragement.[2] Douglas' classmates later joked that he had been the "first cadet whose mother went through the Academy with him." She apparently exercised an enormous influence upon his career. In 1935, the fifty-five-year-old Chief of Staff of the United States Army eagerly asked his eighty-two-year-old mother if he should accept a position in the Philippines. "Shall I go? Shall I take the post?" She replied imperiously: "I want you to do it, Doug-y," adding: "I feel that it is ordained that you go, and that it will lead you to an even greater role." Douglas later recalled that his close relationship with his mother was "one of the dominant factors of my life."[3]

[2] One message that his mother sent to him read:
Do you know that your soul is of my soul such a part
That you seem to be fiber and core of my heart?
None other can pain me as you, son, can do;
None other can please me or praise me as you.
Remember the world will be quick with its blame
If shadow or shame ever darken your name.
Like mother, like son, is saying so true
The world will judge largely of mother by you.
Be this then your task, if task it shall be
To force this proud world to do homage to me.
Be sure it will say, when its verdict you've won
She reaps as she sowed: "This man is her son!"

[3] Amateur psychoanalysts may one day find much of interest in this relationship. "Pinky" MacArthur kept Douglas' brown hair in curls and dressed him in skirts until he was eight years old. Although Douglas developed a normal interest in girls, his first marriage ended in divorce. His wife complained about his performance "in the boudoir," and declared: "It was an interfering mother-in-law who eventually succeeded in disrupting our married life." Douglas' second marriage, at

Douglas MacArthur passed his childhood years on the western frontier posts where his father was stationed. His first recollection, he was fond of saying, was "the sound of Army bugles." For a young boy, it was an exciting and adventurous existence, replete with Indians, outlaws, and hardbitten cavalrymen. He was a poor student, less concerned with formal education than with the military environment around him. "I learned to ride and shoot even before I could read or write," he recalled, "indeed almost before I could walk and talk." In 1899, he enrolled at West Point. There, spurred by his family tradition, his background, and his own keen interest, he compiled a brilliant academic record. When he graduated in 1903, he was first in his class, with the highest scholastic average in the preceding quarter-century.

MacArthur embarked for the Philippines on his first military assignment as second lieutenant of engineers. In 1904, he interrupted his surveys of roads and harbors to join his father's staff in Japan. Here he mingled with the Japanese military, and carefully noted their capabilities. Shortly thereafter, he began a nine-months tour of the Far East as his father's aide-de-camp. It was "the most important training of my entire life," he later noted. "Here was western civilization's last earth frontier. It was crystal clear to me that the future and, indeed, the very existence of America, were irrevocably entwined with Asia and its land outposts." MacArthur never lost his Kiplingesque view that the West would redeem the East, nor his assurance that he had a unique capacity for understanding what he termed "the Oriental mind." His destiny, he believed, lay in Asia. "Its mystic hold," he wrote, was "always . . . upon me."

But ambitious young officers must make certain sacrifices and MacArthur reluctantly deferred his assumption of the "White Man's Burden" by returning to the United States to pursue his career. In 1906, he became military aide to President Theodore Roosevelt, whose views on foreign policy he much admired. In 1913, he was appointed to the General Staff, and the following year took part in the American occupation of Vera Cruz. The First World War, however, gave him his greatest opportunity thus far to display his military talents. In 1917, he proposed to President Woodrow Wilson that National Guard

---

age fifty-seven, occurred shortly after his mother's death, and bore him his only child nine months later. "One of General MacArthur's favorite photographs of his mother," according to the caption at the MacArthur Memorial in Norfolk, Virginia, shows "Pinky" MacArthur gazing upon a photo of Douglas in full military uniform, which she cradles in her arm.

troops be sent to France. When this "Rainbow Division" was formed, composed of crack units from different states, MacArthur became its best-known leader and eventually its commanding officer. The overseas fighting soon revealed MacArthur as an outstanding combat officer, and he garnered numerous medals. The press also began to follow the exploits of the daring young officer, who carried a riding crop and attired himself in a bright turtle neck sweater and flowing muffler under a loose field jacket. He was quickly dubbed "The d'Artagnon of the A.E.F.," and by others, "The Beau Brummel of the A.E.F."

After the war, MacArthur became Superintendent of West Point— the youngest in more than a century. The United States Military Academy was then behind the times and tradition-bound, and Mac-Arthur worked to reform and revitalize it. In 1922, shortly after mar-rying Louise Cromwell Brooks, a lively and wealthy divorcee, he was "exiled" to the Philippines by traditionalists in the War Department, anxious to rid West Point of a meddlesome reformer. MacArthur was not displeased by his return to the Orient, but the new Mrs. Mac-Arthur grew increasingly despondent. Accustomed to a dazzling social life, she found the general's spartan existence intolerable, and com-plained to friends that life in Manila was "extremely dull." In 1929, she divorced MacArthur, remarking: "We were wholly incompatible." The following year, when MacArthur was offered the coveted post of Chief of Staff of the United States Army, he accepted the return to Washington somewhat reluctantly. "My first inclination was to try and beg off," he noted. "But my mother . . . sensed what was in my mind and cabled me to accept. She said my father would be ashamed if I showed timidity. That settled it."

As Chief of Staff from 1930 to 1935, MacArthur found himself at cross purposes with critics of the armed forces. He frequently de-nounced pacifists in public statements, often pairing them with Com-munists, and grew furious at proposals for reducing the size of the American military. On the campus he was booed as a warmonger, while in Congress he was denounced as "a polished popinjay." When President Roosevelt suggested a cut in the military budget to Mac-Arthur, the Chief of Staff became incensed and, as he later wrote, "said something to the general effect that when we lost the next war, and an American boy, lying in the mud with an enemy bayonet through his belly and an enemy foot on his dying throat, spat out his last curse, I wanted the name not to be MacArthur, but Roose-velt." The President grew enraged in turn, and MacArthur apologized. As they left the executive mansion, the Secretary of War told Mac-

Arthur, "You've saved the Army." MacArthur recalled that "I just vomited on the steps of the White House."

The interwar years were especially distressing for MacArthur because, after all, what is a great general without a war? In the dreary, practical world of the thirties, preoccupied with economic disaster and social reform, MacArthur turned hungrily for spiritual sustenance to fond memories of past wars. What had happened, he wondered, to the glory of the Great War? His public speeches, replete with colorful descriptions of armed combat, easily surpassed in glamour his humdrum Washington existence as Chief of Staff of an Army that did not fight.

Actually, however, the Army did fight one battle in those otherwise uneventful years, and ironically it was against the aging soldiers of World War I. In the grim days of June, 1932, thousands of veterans massed in Washington to petition Congress for early payment of their war service bonuses. Encamped in a miserable shantytown on the Anacostia Flats, they lived peacefully with their wives and families. When President Hoover ordered the camp cleared, MacArthur donned his most dashing uniform, seized his riding crop, mounted his horse, and rode off to take personal command. He ordered out four troops of cavalry with drawn sabers, six tanks, and a column of infantry with fixed bayonets. These forces easily routed the startled squatters through use of tear gas and bayonets, and put the torch to their encampment. Through the night men, women, and children, their eyes streaming with tears, coughed, choked, and staggered frantically from their burning tents through the darkness into the safety of Maryland. Many were clubbed or bayonetted, and a baby died from inhaling the tear gas fumes. Outrage at the incident was widespread. The Baltimore *Sun* declared that MacArthur had engaged in "military romanticism undefiled, bare of the tiniest alloy of common sense." MacArthur countered by claiming that the "mob" was "animated by the essence of revolution." In later years, he maintained that he had narrowly averted a Communist revolution, and that criticism of his actions represented "the beginning of a definite and ceaseless campaign" to destroy him by "the Communists and their friends."

His tenure as Chief of Staff at an end, MacArthur departed again in 1935 for the Philippines to become the top military advisor for this Far Eastern outpost of America's colonial empire. Upon entering his air-conditioned penthouse atop the luxurious Manila Hotel, he left his Washington critics behind and assumed the lordly status still enjoyed by white generals in the Orient. Appointed Field Marshall at his own insistence in 1936, MacArthur earned a salary higher than Manuel Quezon, President of the Republic, and he participated in ceremonies of high pomp and splendor. The *Army and Navy Journal* described him at one parade, standing next to the President, "in a white uniform of his own design made of sharkskin material, with four stars on his shoulder, a red ribbon at the base of his lapels, and his General Staff insignia on his left breast." Critics at home also noted his gaudy "scrambled egg" cap, and began referring to him as "the Napoleon of Luzon." In 1937, he married Jean Marie Faircloth— like his mother, the scion of an old Southern military family—and this marriage was long and happy. MacArthur was right: life in the Orient was indeed rich. "I am here by the Grace of God," he proclaimed. "This is my destiny."

And yet, MacArthur faced a formidable task in making the Philippines defensible against military attack. American generals had warned that it was impossible. MacArthur was more optimistic, however, and presented a plan to Quezon in 1936 for development of the islands' defenses over the next decade. "I am certain," he told army officers, "that no chancellery in the world . . . will ever willingly make an effort to willfully attack the Philippines after the present development has been completed." And despite the target date of 1946, he grew increasingly confident of the islands' military power in the intervening years. After the Second World War had begun in Europe, he predicted that an attack upon the Philippines would cost the invader casualties of more than half a million men and resources of more than five billion dollars. Moreover, he was far from certain that the Japanese would want to invade the Philippines. "It has been assumed," he declared in 1939, "in my opinion, erroneously, that Japan covets these Islands. Just why has never been satisfactorily explained. Proponents of such a theory fail fully to credit the logic of the Japanese mind."

It was with considerable dismay, then, that MacArthur saw the Japanese invade the Philippines in 1941, smash his fragile forces, and occupy the islands. The most devastating blow came nine hours after the bombing of Pearl Harbor, when, despite warnings of an attack, MacArthur was caught by the Japanese with his planes on the ground, some wing tip to wing tip. Two waves of Japanese bombers and fighter planes virtually destroyed the American air force in the Philippines—the most formidable American air unit outside the United States. After the Japanese invasion of the islands, several weeks of bitter fighting ensued, and American and Filipino troops retreated to the Bataan peninsula. MacArthur retired to the island fortress of Corregidor, from which he directed military operations. The situation quickly became hopeless—so hopeless, indeed, that at one point MacArthur told Washington that he supported President Quezon's plan for neutralization, rather than defense, of the Philippines. Because MacArthur delayed in calling for the retreat to Bataan, the peninsula was poorly stocked with food and other vital supplies; the troops, placed on half-rations at their arrival, soon found circumstances deteriorating to the point of slow starvation.

Ordered by Roosevelt to withdraw from the Philippines to take command of American forces in Australia, MacArthur reluctantly agreed, encouraged by the hope that he might thereby help relieve the garrison at Bataan. On the night of March 11, 1942, accompanied by his wife, child, the child's Chinese nurse, and the fourteen officers from his staff later known as the "Bataan gang," [4] he set out on a daring trip through the Pacific by PT boat. Upon his arrival in Australia, he announced: "I came through, and I shall return." When the Office of War Information suggested changing the phrase to "we shall return," MacArthur refused to hear of it. The units remaining on Bataan and Corregidor[5] fought bravely for another two months until, exhausted and starving, they finally surrendered themselves and the Philippines to the Japanese.

MacArthur took command of the Southwest Pacific region, determined to shatter Japanese military might and to retake the Philippines—"the main objective of my planning from the time of my departure from Corregidor." At the outset, he was badly hampered by shortages of manpower and supplies—shortages that he believed were consequences of a deliberate effort to weaken his command. The Navy, the Air Force, General George Marshall, Harry Hopkins, and the British government all aroused his ire, and he wavered in his views on President Roosevelt. His staff, particularly the "Bataan gang," became petulant and resentful at what they regarded as attempts by MacArthur's personal and political enemies at home to destroy him. Gradually, however, MacArthur's forces turned the tide of battle. In New Guinea and throughout the Pacific they engaged in the series of brilliant amphibious operations that contributed greatly to American victory. "Yes, we've come a long way," he told a visitor in 1944,

[4] This was actually a misnomer, since their work had not been at the front in Bataan, but in the secluded tunnel headquarters on Corregidor.

[5] All of which MacArthur recommended for citations except the Marine and Naval detachments, which he thought had received sufficient glory in World War I.

"despite the Navy cabal that hates me, and the New Deal cabal." MacArthur proved himself to be a superb commander and tactician, and, bolstered by a feverish effort on the part of his public relations staff, his reputation grew accordingly.

But MacArthur could not forget the Philippines. In mid-1944, he and other military leaders were summoned to a conference at Pearl Harbor with President Roosevelt, who wanted their views on future strategy in the Pacific. Naval spokesmen urged by-passing the Philippines and attacking Formosa—a plan to which MacArthur strenuously objected. Downgrading the military significance of Formosa—an island which several years later he proclaimed of supreme importance—he argued persuasively for the liberation of the Philippines. When Roosevelt adopted the MacArthur strategy, the general was so overjoyed that he warmed a bit toward the New Deal leader. "The President is a man of great vision," he told a reporter, "once things are explained to him." MacArthur's moment of glory drew nigh. In October, he went in with the third invasion wave at Leyte beach, delivering his prepared address into a microphone: "People of the Philippines: I have returned. . . . Rally to me. . . . The guidance of Divine God points the way. Follow in His Name to the Holy Grail of Righteous Victory." The Japanese surrender to MacArthur on September 2, 1945 in Tokyo Bay was almost anticlimactic.

At the end of the Second World War, President Harry Truman appointed MacArthur Supreme Commander for the Allied Powers in Japan (SCAP). The general settled down with his family in the American Embassy in Tokyo, and drove downtown every day through the traffic-stilled streets to the Dai-Ichi building, from which he directed the reconstruction of Japanese society. His power in Japan was virtually complete; he ignored the Allied Council and maintained distant relations with the State Department. Fortunately for the Japanese, his rule proved unexpectedly benign and remarkably reformist. SCAP encouraged civil liberties, democratic institutions, land reform, women's suffrage, religious freedom, disarmament, a purge of prewar leaders, and, for a time, the labor movement. Sitting back and puffing on his corncob pipe, MacArthur expressed his pride in the Occupation's accomplishments. "It is fascinating to go back and read Plato's vision of Utopia," he told a reporter, "and to see how far we have progressed."

After 1948, however, the reformist impulses of the Occupation began to ebb. One early goal—the breakup of the *Zaibatsu*, the monopolistic Japanese trusts that MacArthur rather curiously viewed as practicing "a kind of private socialism"—rapidly deteriorated as economic recovery eclipsed economic reform in the minds of the Occupation authorities. The abolition of Japanese military forces, hailed by MacArthur at the outset of the Occupation, gave American policymakers cause for regret as the Cold War heightened, and a paramilitary national police force was created to fill the gap. News correspondents had constant difficulties if their stories or newspaper's editorial policies departed from the SCAP line. MacArthur began repressing dissident left-wing politicians, newspapers, and trade unions. But the sour conclusion of the Occupation should not detract from MacArthur's overall success in reforming many of the archaic and reactionary institutions in Japanese life.

While still in Japan, MacArthur made his most serious attempt to gain the GOP Presidential nomination. Throughout the 1940s, his political prospects had been promoted by the Hearst press, the Scripps-Howard papers, and the Chicago *Tribune*. In 1944, Senator Arthur Vandenberg had attempted to secure the Republican nomination for MacArthur, but had seen his campaign destroyed by the untimely publication of Nebraska Congressman A. L. Miller's correspondence with the general.[6] Encouraged again by his friends at home and by his staff in Japan, MacArthur entered the Wisconsin Presidential primary in 1948. Senator Joseph McCarthy—who in later years would be one of the general's most avid supporters—strongly backed MacArthur's opponent, Harold Stassen, and mailed his constituents a letter criticizing the general's age and alluding to his divorce. In the primary, MacArthur garnered only eight delegates of Wisconsin's twenty-seven, and his Presidential boom immediately collapsed. At the GOP national convention, he received only eleven of 1094 votes on the first ballot; on the third, Governor Thomas E. Dewey of New York won the nomination.

On June 27, 1950, shortly after the outbreak of hostilities in Korea, President Truman ordered MacArthur and his forces in Japan to defend South Korea against the invasion from the north. MacArthur deployed his forces in a pattern of slow retreat, seeking to win time for the arrival of United Nations detachments, which were gradually added to his command. In September, driven to the southern tip of the peninsula, but reinforced by fresh troops, he launched a brilliant

---

[6] "Unless this New Deal can be stopped this time, our American way of life is forever doomed," the Nebraska Congressman maintained. MacArthur replied: "I do unreservedly agree with the complete wisdom and statesmanship of your comments."

attack behind the enemy lines at Inchon, which routed the North Korean armies and lay the groundwork for his advance north. By October, MacArthur's forces controlled all of South Korea and much of North Korea. President Truman flew to Wake Island to confer with the general, who assured him that there was "very little" chance of Chinese intervention. Four days after the Wake Island meeting, Mac-Arthur flew triumphantly into Pyongyang, the North Korean capitol. In an apparent reference to North Korean Premier Kim Il-Sung, he asked jocularly: "Have you got any celebrities to greet me? What about Kim Buck Too?" On November 24, despite several weeks of contact with Chinese units, he ordered his troops on to the Yalu in an "end the war offensive," promising that they would be home by Christmas. He remained confident of victory. As he stated several months earlier: "It is in the pattern of Oriental psychology to respect and follow aggressive, resolute and dynamic leadership."

The intervention of several hundred thousand Chinese troops at this point therefore came as a shock to MacArthur, as well as to his forces, who went reeling in bloody and disorderly retreat for 250 miles.[7] Driven south of the thirty-eighth parallel once again, the infuriated MacArthur demanded that the war be extended to the "privileged sanctuary" of China through American bombing missions, blockade of the China coast, and the use of Generalissimo Chiang Kai-shek's forces. The Truman Administration, embarrassed at home and abroad by his public outbursts, sought to silence him, but to no avail. In a telegram to House Republican leader Joseph W. Martin, Jr., which the legislator read on the floor of Congress, MacArthur again called for the use of Chinese Nationalist troops. "It seems strangely difficult for some to realize that here in Asia is where the Communist conspirators have elected to make their play for global conquest," he explained. "There is no substitute for victory." On April 11, exasperated by this latest in a long series of inflammatory statements, President Truman relieved him of his commands.

MacArthur and his staff reacted bitterly to his dismissal. "Moscow and Peiping rejoiced. The bells were rung and a holiday atmosphere prevailed. The left wingers everywhere exulted," he wrote years later. Once again he blamed insidious forces at home for his humiliation. Discussing his career in the Pacific from 1941 to 1951, he remarked: "I have always felt that my real enemy was behind me—in Washington—not in front of me." On the other hand, all was not lost. The

---

[7] MacArthur later observed in irritation that the U.S. Army's "skillful withdrawal had been accomplished with such speed that it led to many comments by ignorant correspondents that the troops were in flight."

decision to remove him from command "was the judgment of one individual." [8] When he returned to America, he would rally the people to his side and be vindicated. He would expose the Truman Administration's policy of "appeasement." "Destiny," he declared, "is sending me home to tell the people the truth."

Amidst the ballyhoo of his return to America, MacArthur labored assiduously to make his case. In his speeches to public officials and to the enormous welcoming crowds, he denied that he had been insubordinate to his Commander-in-Chief, and assailed the Truman Administration's Korean policy. "There is no policy—there is nothing, I tell you, no plan, or anything," he told a Senate hearing. Truman and his advisors were delivering Asia to Communism. "Appeasement," he informed the Massachusetts legislature, had become "the policy of war on the battlefield." Truman and his supporters lashed back, in turn, at MacArthur. The general had deliberately defied Presidential authority, they argued, and had given the President no choice but to dismiss him. Moreover, his foreign policy proposals raised grave risks of igniting World War III.

However, the attempt by Truman supporters to portray the conflict between the general and the President as a struggle between advocates of war and peace is more than a little disingenuous. It was, after all, Truman—and not MacArthur—who set the United States policy of support for Chiang Kai-shek against his domestic foes, until the cause seemed hopeless; who sent American troops into Korea without consulting Congress; who escalated the aim of American intervention in Korea from defense of South Korean independence to destruction of North Korean independence;[9] who prevented the successful conclusion

[8] Years later he wrote witheringly: "I had heard much of President Truman's violent temper and paroxysms of ungovernable rage."

[9] On September 11, Truman had authorized MacArthur's invasion of North Korea, and on September 30, U.S. Ambassador Warren Austin presented the U.S. position to the U.N.: "The aggressor's forces should not be permitted to have refuge behind an imaginary line. . . . The artificial barrier which has divided North and South Korea has no basis for existence in law or in reason." This reasoning, of course, makes it difficult to understand how the North Koreans could have been branded international aggressors in the first place. It also bears a striking similarity to that used by MacArthur when he called for the bombing of that "privileged sanctuary," China. Eventually, the United States government adopted the goal of "liberating" the North and placing it under the authority of the South Korean government. India and six other Afro-Asian nations complained that it seemed hypocritical to "authorize the unification of Korea by force against North Korea after North Korea's attempt to unify Korea by force against South Korea." American policy had changed a great deal since Secretary of State Acheson's statement of July 10, 1950, declaring that the U.S. fought in Korea "solely for restoring the Republic of Korea [South Korea] to its status prior to the invasion from the North."

of the Chinese revolution by sending the Seventh Fleet to defend the Nationalist garrison on Formosa; who refused to recognize the government of mainland China; who resumed aid to the Generalissimo in 1950, thereby reviving that dictator's fading dreams of reconquering the mainland. And when Chinese Communist leaders, assessing the direction of these actions, warned publically that China would not "supinely tolerate the destruction of its neighbor," and privately relayed a similar message through the Indian government, the President refused to modify his plans for the conquest of North Korea. After China intervened, and the war in the Far East raged ever more fiercely, laying waste to Korea and taking an estimated four million casualties, it was not entirely surprising that MacArthur would urge the utilization of Chiang's troops or would suggest the bombing of mainland China. To claim that the general's policies were warlike and foolhardy is, in retrospect, no longer sufficient. They must also be placed in the context of American policy in Asia, which was already aggressive enough to plunge the nation into a third world war—even without MacArthur.

To be sure, there were subtle differences between Truman's policies and those of MacArthur. The general would have embraced Chiang to a greater extent than did Truman. He would also have been willing to sacrifice some of the goodwill of America's allies. On the other hand, MacArthur, unlike Truman, did not publicly threaten the use of the atomic bomb against the Chinese. And yet, these were but shadings in the overall American foreign policy of a worldwide offensive against Communism. The general claimed to be confused as to how his statements radically departed from those made by the Truman administration, and there is more than a little substance to his claim. The irony in the confrontation between the general and the President, then, was not that MacArthur sounded like a warhawk, which he was, but that Truman emerged as a spokesman for peace, which he was not.[10]

MacArthur had predicted in his April, 1951 speech to Congress that he would "just fade away," but his political activities continued for more than a year. Setting up his home base in a suite at New York's Waldorf Towers, where his aide, General Courtney Whitney, turned out "communiqués" from "GHQ," MacArthur travelled the country to alert Americans to the perils they faced. In the summer of

---

[10] It is revealing to compare the reactions of the two men to the Vietnam War. Truman consistently supported the escalation of American military activities in Vietnam, while MacArthur urged withdrawal of American troops in 1961.

1952, he addressed the Republican National Convention, and lambasted the Truman Administration amidst thunderous applause. That December, President-elect Eisenhower met with MacArthur to discuss the Korean War. MacArthur advocated a peace conference, which, if unsuccessful, would be followed by "the atomic bombing of enemy military concentrations and installations in North Korea and the sowing of fields of suitable radio-active materials," the bombing of China, and the landing of Chinese Nationalist troops in Manchuria to overthrow the Communist government. To his chagrin, MacArthur was not consulted again. Indeed, he later complained that, after retirement, he was "never consulted by my government about the Far East, an area which I know and understand better than any living American."

Perhaps aware that his political appeal was ebbing, MacArthur accepted a post as chairman of the board of the Remington Rand Corporation in August, 1952. In his new role as a businessman, he emerged as a spokesman for conservative economic interests. In 1954, for example, he delivered what one of his aides described as "a stirring defense of the capitalistic system" to the National Association of Manufacturers. His memoirs, written shortly before his death, warn readers of devious Marxist plots and proposals, among them the Federal Income Tax Law of 1914. "Most officials of our government over the past years will deny . . . any intent to establish in this nation the basis for the emergence of a Socialistic, much less a Communist state," he argued, "but the course of fiscal policy has done just that."

In the last years of his life, shaken by illness, MacArthur grew gaunt and haggard. For the first time, he looked his age. And yet, a few bright moments remained. On the fifteenth anniversary of Philippine independence, he made his last trip to the Far East to attend the ceremonies as a guest of the island nation. "I visited again the old historic spots," he wrote, "the white beaches of Leyte . . . the rugged slopes of Corregidor gone back to jungle, the hills of Bataan under the shadows of the setting sun." The political road had failed MacArthur, but the memories of his military past lived on. In May, 1962, he told the Corps of Cadets in an emotional speech at West Point: "When I cross the river my last conscious thoughts will be of the Corps—and the Corps—and the Corps." A soldier to the end, he died in the Army's Walter Reed Hospital on April 5, 1964.

MacArthur was an intelligent, articulate, handsome, and talented officer, whose major flaws—his vanity and his promotion of right-wing, nationalistic causes—should not be allowed to overshadow his accomplishments. Few would deny him the place he has earned among the foremost generals and political figures in American history. And yet, as Roosevelt sensed in 1932, there was something fundamentally unhealthy about the general's rise to fame and power. For in normal times—when men till the soil, mine the ore, work in factories and offices, and, occasionally, search for truth and beauty—the martial virtues are ignored. It is only when a nation enters a time of war and sustained military crisis that citizens rush to place laurels upon their generals. MacArthur's meteoric career, his extraordinary political influence, and his potential for Caesarism all attest to America's steady growth in the twentieth century toward the Garrison State.

Chronology of the Life of MacArthur

1880   (January 26) Born in Little Rock, Arkansas, the son of Arthur and Mary MacArthur.

1885–89   Attends public and private schools in Arkansas, New Mexico, Texas, Missouri, and the District of Columbia.

1895–97   Cadet at West Texas Military Academy.

1899–1903 Attends United States Military Academy at West Point. Graduates first in his class.

1903   Commissioned Second Lieutenant, Corps of Engineers, and assigned to Philippines.

1904   Promoted to First Lieutenant.

1905   Aide-de-Camp to his father, Major General Arthur MacArthur, in Tokyo.

1906   Aide-de-Camp to President Theodore Roosevelt.

1911   Promoted to Captain.

1913   Member of the General Staff, Washington, D.C.

1914   Participates in Vera Cruz expedition.

1915   Promoted to Major.

1917   (August) Promoted to Colonel.
(September) Chief of Staff, 42nd (Rainbow) Division, American Expeditionary Forces in France.

1918   Promoted to Brigadier General.

1918   Commanding General, 42nd Division, France and Germany.

1919–22   Superintendent, United States Military Academy at West Point.

1922   Marries Mrs. Louise Cromwell Brooks.

1924   Commanding General, Philippine Division.

1925   Promoted to Major General.

1927   President, American Olympic Committee.

1929   Divorces his first wife.

1930   Promoted to General.

1930–35   Chief of Staff, United States Army.

1932   Routs the Bonus Expeditionary Force at Anacostia Flats.

1936–41   Field Marshal of the Philippine Army.

1937   Marries Jean Marie Faircloth.

1938   The general's only child, Arthur MacArthur, is born.

1941	(July) Recalled to active service and named Commanding General, United States Army forces in the Far East. (December) Japanese attack Pearl Harbor and invade the Philippines.
1942	(March) Abandons the Philippines for Australia. (April) Named Supreme Commander, Southwest Pacific Area.
1944	American forces land at Leyte Beach. MacArthur returns to the Philippines.
1945	Japanese government surrenders. MacArthur named Supreme Commander for the Allied Powers in Japan.
1948	Enters Republican Presidential primary in Wisconsin.
1950	(June) Korean War begins. MacArthur named Commanding General, United Nations command. (September) Landing at Inchon. (October) Wake Island meeting with President Harry S. Truman. (November) Chinese enter Korean War.
1951	Truman relieves MacArthur of his commands. MacArthur returns to the United States, addresses a joint session of Congress, and campaigns against the Truman Administration's foreign policy.
1952	Appointed Chairman of the Board, Remington Rand Corporation.
1961	Revisits the Philippines.
1964	(April 5) Dies at Walter Reed Hospital, Washington, D.C.

PART ONE

DOUGLAS MACARTHUR LOOKS AT THE WORLD

1

A New Look at West Point (1920)[1]

As Superintendent of the United States Military Academy at West Point from 1919 to 1922, MacArthur sought to reform the institution and to expand the size of its student body. The following are excerpts from his first annual report of June 30, 1920.

My assumption of the command of the United States Military Academy synchronized with the ending of an epoch in the life of this Institution. With the termination of the World War the mission of West Point at once became the preparation of officer personnel for the next possible future war. The methods of training here have always been largely influenced by the purpose of producing the type of officer which the Army at large dictated. The excellence with which the Academy's mission has been carried out in the past has been testified on the battlefields of the world for a hundred years and more. The problem which faced the authorities was, therefore, this: Have new conditions developed, have the lessons of the World War indicated that a changed type of officer was necessary in order to produce the maximum of efficiency in the handling of men at arms? West Point, existing solely as a source of supply and a feeder to the Army, if a new era faces the latter, West Point must of necessity train its personnel accordingly.

In meeting this problem those who were charged with the solution undertook the task with a full realization of its seriousness. It was well understood that it was no light affair to attempt even in moderate degree to modify a status which had proved itself so splendidly for a century and more. It was understood that change under the guise of

[1] Reprinted by permission of the Bureau of Archives, MacArthur Memorial.

reconstruction was destructive unless clearly and beyond question it introduced something of added benefit. It was recognized that reform to be effective must be evolutionary and not revolutionary. It was evident that many sources of help, in the nature of advice and consultation, lay outside of the Military Academy in the persons of distinguished officers of the Army at large and of professional educators throughout the country.

Careful analysis yielded the following conclusions: Until the World War armed conflicts between nations had been fought by comparatively a small fraction of the populations involved. These professional armies were composed very largely of elements which frequently required the most rigid methods of training, the severest forms of discipline, to weld them into a flexible weapon for use on the battlefield. Officers were, therefore, developed to handle a more or less recalcitrant element along definite and simple lines, and a fixed psychology resulted. Early in the World War it was realized to the astonishment of both sides that the professional armies, upon which they had relied, were unable to bring the combat to a definite decision. It became evident, due largely to the elaborate and rapid methods of communication and transportation which had grown up in the past generation, that national communities had become so intimate, that war was a condition which involved the efforts of every man, woman, and child in the countries affected. War had become a phenomenon which truly involved the nation in arms. Personnel was of necessity improvised, both at the front and at the rear; the magnitude of the effort, both of supply and of combat, was so great that individuals were utilized with the minimum of training. In general result, this was largely offset by the high personal type of those engaged. Discipline no longer required extreme methods. Men generally needed only to be told what to do, rather than to be forced by the fear of consequence of failure. The great numbers involved made it impossible to apply the old rigid methods which had been so successful when battle lines were not so extensive. The rule of this war can but apply to that of the future. Improvisation will be the watchword. Such changed conditions will require a modification in type of the officer, a type possessing all of the cardinal military virtues as of yore, but possessing an intimate understanding of the mechanics of human feelings, a comprehensive grasp of world and national affairs, and a liberalization of conception which amounts to a change in his psychology of command. This standard became the basis of the construction of the new West Point in the spirit of old West Point.

To hold fast to those policies typified in the motto of the Academy —"Duty, Honor, Country"—to cling to thoroughness as to a lodestar, to continue to inculcate the habit of industry, to implant as of old the gospel of cleanliness—to be clean, to live clean, and to think clean —and yet to introduce a new atmosphere of liberalization in doing away with provincialism, a substitution of subjective for objective discipline, a progressive increase of cadet responsibility tending to develop initiative and force of character rather than automatic performance of stereotyped functions, to broaden the curriculum so as to be abreast of the best modern thought on education, to bring West Point into a new and closer relationship with the Army at large, has been the aim and purpose of my administration throughout the past year.

The details of the changes that have been brought about in conformity with the above policy are to be found in the report of the Academic Board on a change in the curriculum and in the reports of the various heads of bureaus, which I incorporate in the body of this report.

The results have transcended my most sanguine expectation; they will be felt throughout the Army at large with the graduation of the classes now under tuition.

The problem which I have discussed above, important as it is, dwarfs into insignificance before the real question of reconstruction that confronts this Institution. It is one of quantity rather than quality. The Reorganization Bill of June 4th practically doubled the size of the officer personnel of the Regular Army, but failed utterly to provide an increase in the supply thereof. The Military Academy was left with the same authorized strength of 1,334 cadets that it had had previously. It cannot now supply more than one-third of our officers even in times of peace. In contrast with this condition I invite attention to the fact that the Brigade of Midshipmen has now an authorization of 3,136 members to supply a commissioned personnel of the Navy of approximately 5,000. I regard a commensurate increase in the Corps of Cadets as the most necessary and constructive feature of a sound military policy that confronts the Nation today. I have recommended elsewhere legislation designed to double the strength of the Corps of Cadets, the increase to be assimilated in four annual increments, the necessary construction to be undertaken in consonance therewith. The cost of the new installations entailed thereby would amount to approximately $12 million, to be appropriated at the rate of $3 million for four years. In making this recommendation I wish to emphasize the comparatively small appropriations that have been made for construction at this Institution since its foundation in 1802. The total sum is something less than $20 million. Many of our State institutions, relying entirely on taxation within their own States, have more than doubled this amount during a much shorter life. I am informed that the yearly budget of many is more than twice that of the Military Academy. When I draw attention to the fact that the University of Chicago has from one beneficiary received more than $50 million in his lifetime, that within the last year $15 million has been left by one bequest to Princeton University, some idea will be obtained of the comparative indigence with which this school has been faced. The press has recently stated that $212 million is being sought for this year by the universities of the country for still further expansion of plant.

I bespeak a broad and mature consideration of the question lest a condition may ultimately result which will be paid for in the bitterness of American blood. . . .

2
A Critique of Christian Pacifism (1931)[1]

When the religious pacifist journal, The World To-morrow, *conducted an opinion poll of Protestant clergymen in 1931, 12,076 of the 19,372 respondents maintained that the Christian Church should refuse to sanction war. MacArthur, when asked his views on their response, sent this letter on June 2, 1931.*

I appreciate very much the courtesy of the suggestion contained in your note of April 20, and am glad, indeed, to avail myself of the privilege of commenting on the general subject of the Church in war.

My predominant feeling with reference to the majority of the replies received by your paper from 19,372 clergymen is that of surprise. Surprise at the knowledge that so many of the clergymen of our country have placed themselves on record as repudiating in advance the constitutional obligations that will fall upon them equally with all other elements of our citizenship in supporting this country in case of need.

To exercise privilege without assuming attendant responsibility and obligation is to occupy a position of license, a position apparently sought by men who do not hesitate to avail themselves of the privileges conferred by our democracy upon its citizens, but who, in effect, proclaim their willingness to see this nation perish rather than participate in its defense.

The question of war and peace is one that rests, under our form of Government, in Congress. In exercising this authority, Congress voices the will of the majority, whose right to rule is the cornerstone upon which our governmental edifice is built. Under the Constitution, its pronouncement on such a question is final, and is obligatory upon every citizen of the United States.

That men who wear the cloth of the Church should openly defend repudiation of the laws of the land, with the necessary implications and ramifications arising from such a general attitude toward our statutes, seems almost unbelievable. It will certainly hearten every

[1] From "Reverberations!" *The World Tomorrow,* XIV (June, 1931): 192–93.

potential or actual criminal and malefactor who either has or contemplates breaking some other law.

Anomalous as it seems, it apparently stamps the clergyman as a leading exponent of law violation at individual pleasure.

I am mindful of the right accorded every American citizen to endeavor by lawful means to secure such changes in the Constitution or statutes as he may desire. But to concede to him the right to defy existing law is to recognize a state of anarchy and the collapse of properly constituted authority.

May I remark also that, if we acknowledge the prerogative of the individual to disregard the obligations placed upon him by American citizenship, it seems only logical to ask him to forego all rights guaranteed by such citizenship.

It also surprises me that while apparently entering a plea for freedom of conscience, these clergymen are attempting to dictate to the consciences of those who honestly differ from them over questions of national defense.

Their sentiments and implied efforts are injecting the Church into the affairs of State and endangering the very principle that they claim to uphold.

Perhaps the greatest privilege of our country, which indeed was the genius of its foundation, is religious freedom. Religious freedom, however, can exist only so long as government survives. To render our country helpless would invite destruction, not only of our political and economic freedom, but also of our religion.

Another surprise comes in the revelation that so many seem to be unfamiliar with the struggle of mankind for the free institutions that we enjoy.

Magna Charta, the Declaration of Independence, the Emancipation, the rights of small nations and other birthrights of this generation have been bought with the high price of human suffering and human sacrifice, much of it on the fields of battle.

I am surprised that men of clear and logical minds confuse defensive warfare with the disease which it alone can cure when all other remedies have failed.

Do they not know that police systems and armed national defense are the human agencies made necessary by the deep-seated disease of individual depravity, the menace of personal greed and hatred?

Should not these clergymen turn their attention to the individual sinner and rid the country of crime rather than attack the national keepers of the peace, the most potent governmental agency yet devised for this very purpose?

It is a distinct disappointment to know that men who are called to wield the sword of the spirit are deluded into believing that the mechanical expedient of disarming men will transform hatred into love and selfishness into altruism.

May I also express surprise that some have lost sight of the fact that in none of our past wars have clergymen been required to bear arms, and that under the terms of the Geneva Convention, ratified by the United States in 1907 (Sec. 130 and 132), chaplains are non-combatants and not authorized to bear arms.

And if United States Army chaplains are ever guilty of using inflammatory propaganda, such activity is without warrant of authority by any statute or order ever promulgated in the history of the country.

Perhaps I should also remind them that, under the terms of the League of Nations, the United States would be required to maintain a standing army of at least a half-million men in order to be able to carry out its mandates.

I am curious to know how many of the clergymen who voted for the League have read the articles and understand that under them the peace of the world is to be maintained in the last analysis by armed military forces.

It is difficult to reconcile the faith of these people in the efficacy of newly organized international agencies to keep the peace and enforce respect for international covenants with their self-confessed intention to violate the existing laws of their own long-established government.

A few questions occur to me that could appropriately be asked the clergymen who replied to your questionnaire. In stating that they were in favor of the United States taking the lead in reducing armament even if compelled to make greater proportionate reductions than other countries might be willing to make, did they know that the existing total of our land forces, including regular Army, National Guard and organized reserves, is about one-third of 1 per cent of our population?

Did they know that in other great countries except Germany, whose army is limited by treaty, this ratio is from three to forty-five times as great?

Did they know our total forces in actual size are exceeded by those of at least fifteen other nations, although in population we are exceeded only by Russia, China and India?

Finally, did they consider the words of our Lord as given in the twenty-first verse of the eleventh chapter of St. Luke: "When a strong man armed, keepeth his palace, his goods are in peace"?

In all modesty may I not say to the opponents of national defense that our Lord, who preached the Sermon on the Mount, later in his career declared: "Think not that I am come to send peace on earth. I came not to send peace, but a sword." (St. Matthew, X, 34.)

It is my humble belief that the relation which He came to establish is based upon sacrifice, and that men and women who follow in His train are called by it to the defense of certain priceless principles, even at the cost of their own lives.

And I can think of no principles more high and holy than those for which our national sacrifices have been made in the past. History teaches us that religion and patriotism have always gone hand in hand, while atheism has invariably been accompanied by radicalism, communism, bolshevism, and other enemies of free government.

Have not those who oppose our modest and reasonable efforts for national defense miscalculated the temper and innate spirit of patriotism in the average American?

The fact that our Citizens' Military Training Camps are oversubscribed long before the opening of the camps comforts me that patriotism is still a dominant power in our land.

Any organization which opposes the defense of homeland and the principles hallowed by the blood of our ancestors, which sets up internationalism in the place of patriotism, which teaches the passive submission of right to the forces of the predatory strong, cannot prevail against the demonstrated stanchness of our position.

I confidently believe that a red-blooded and virile humanity which loves peace devotedly, but is willing to die in the defense of the right, is Christian from center to circumference, and will continue to be dominant in the future as in the past.

3

Pacifism and Its Bedfellow, Communism (1932)[1]

On June 8, 1932, MacArthur, then Chief of Staff of the United States Army, made this statement in a commencement address at the University of Pittsburgh. It was received critically by Congress and the press.

Pacifism and its bedfellow, Communism, are all about us. In the theaters, newspapers and magazines, pulpits and lecture halls, schools and colleges, it hangs like a mist before the face of America, organizing the forces of unrest and undermining the morals of the working man.

Day by day this canker eats deeper into the body politic.

For the sentimentalism and emotionalism which have infested our country, we should substitute hard common sense. Pacific habits do not insure peace or immunity from national insult and aggression. Any nation that would keep its self-respect must be prepared to defend itself.

Every reasonable man knows that war is cruel and destructive, and yet very little of the fever of war will melt the veneer of our civilization. History has proved that nations once great, that neglected their national defense are dust and ashes. Where are Rome and Carthage? Where Byzantium? Where Egypt, once so great a state? Where Korea, whose death cries were unheard by the world?

[1] Reprinted by permission of the Bureau of Archives, MacArthur Memorial.

4

Address to the Rainbow Division (1935)[1]

Shortly before his retirement as U.S. Army Chief of Staff, MacArthur addressed the World War I veterans of the 42nd Infantry (Rainbow) Division in Washington on July 14, 1935. His speech combines a striking nostalgia for war with a call to prepare for future combat.

Mr. President and gentlemen of the Rainbow Division, I thank you for the warmth of your greeting. It moves me deeply. It was with you I lived my greatest moments. It is of you I have my greatest memories.

It was seventeen years ago—those days of old have vanished, tone and tint; they have gone glimmering through the dreams of things that were. Their memory is a land where flowers of wondrous beauty and varied colors spring, watered by tears and coaxed and caressed into fuller bloom by the smiles of yesterday. Refrains no longer rise and fall from that land of used-to-be. We listen vainly, but with thirsty ear, for the witching melodies of days that are gone. Ghosts in olive drab and sky blue and German gray pass before our eyes; voices that have stolen away in the echoes from the battlefields no more ring out. The faint, far whisper of forgotten songs no longer floats through the air. Youth, strength, aspirations, struggles, triumphs, despairs, wide winds sweeping, beacons flashing across uncharted depths, movements, vividness, radiance, shadows, faint bugles sounding reveille, far drums beating the long roll, the crash of guns, the rattle of musketry—the still white crosses!

And tonight we are met to remember.

The shadows are lengthening. The division's birthdays are multiplying; we are growing old together. But the story which we commemorate helps us to grow old gracefully. That story is known to all of you. It needs no profuse panegyrics. It is the story of the American soldier of the World War. My estimate of him was formed on the battlefield many years ago and has never changed. I regarded him then, as I regard him now, as one of the world's greatest figures—not

---

[1] Reprinted by permission of the Bureau of Archives, MacArthur Memorial.

only in the era which witnessed his achievements but for all eyes and for all time. I regarded him as not only one of the greatest military figures but also as one of the most stainless; his name and fame are the birthright of every American citizen.

The world's estimate of him will be founded not upon any one battle or even series of battles; indeed, it is not upon the greatest fields of combat or the bloodiest that the recollections of future ages are riveted. The vast theaters of Asiatic conflict are already forgotten today. The slaughtered myriads of Genghis Khan lie in undistinguished graves. Hardly a pilgrim visits the scenes where on the fields of Chalons and Tours the destinies of civilization and Christendom were fixed by the skill of Aetius and the valor of Charles Martel.

The time indeed may come when the memory of the fields of Champagne and Picardy, of Verdun and the Argonne shall be dimmed by the obscurity of revolving years and recollected only as a shadow of ancient days.

But even then the enduring fortitude, the patriotic self-abnegation, and the unsurpassed military genius of the American soldier of the World War will stand forth in undimmed luster; in his youth and strength, his love and loyalty, he gave all that mortality can give. He needs no eulogy from me or from any other man; he has written his own history, and written it in red on his enemy's breast. But when I think of his patience under adversity, of his courage under fire, and of his modesty in victory I am filled with an emotion I cannot express. He belongs to history as furnishing one of the greatest examples of successful and disinterested patriotism. He belongs to posterity as the instructor of future generations in the principles of liberty and right. He belongs to the present—to us—by his glory, by his virtues, and by his achievements.

The memorials of character wrought by him can never be dimmed. He needs no statues or monuments; he has stamped himself in blazing flames upon the souls of his countrymen; he has carved his own statue in the hearts of his people; he has built his own monument in the memory of his compatriots.

The military code which he perpetuates has come down to us from even before the age of knighthood and chivalry. It embraces the highest moral laws and will stand the test of any ethics or philosophies ever promulgated for the uplift of mankind. Its requirements are for the things that are right, and its restraints are from the things that are wrong. Its observance will uplift everyone who comes under its influence. The soldier, above all other men, is required to perform the highest act of religious teaching—sacrifice. In battle and in the face of danger and death he discloses those divine attributes which his Maker gave when He created man in his own image. No physical courage and no brute instincts can take the place of the divine annunciation and spiritual uplift which will alone sustain him. However horrible the incidents of war may be, the soldier who is called upon to offer and to give his life for his country is the noblest development of mankind.

On such an occasion as this my thoughts go back to those men who went with us to their last charge. In memory's eye I can see them now —forming grimly for the attack, blue-lipped, covered with sludge and mud, chilled by the wind and rain of the foxhole, driving home to their objective and to the judgment seat of God. I do not know the dignity of their birth, but I do know the glory of their death. They died unquestioning, uncomplaining, with faith in their hearts and on their lips the hope that we would go on to victory.

Never again for them staggering columns, bending under soggy packs, on many a weary march from dripping dusk to drizzling dawn. Never again will they trudge ankle-deep through the mud on shell-shocked roads. Never again will they stop cursing their luck long enough to whistle through chapped lips a few bars as some clear voice raised the lilt of "Madelon." Never again ghostly trenches, with their maze of tunnels, drifts, pits, dugouts—never again, gentlemen unafraid.

They have gone beyond the mists that blind us here and become part of that beautiful thing we call the Spirit of the Unknown Soldier. In chambered temples of silence the dust of their dauntless valor sleeps, waiting. Waiting in the chancery of Heaven the final reckoning of Judgment Day: "Only those are fit to live who are not afraid to die."

5
Fall of the Philippines (1942)[1]

In response to the news of the surrender of the American garrisons on Bataan and Corregidor to the Japanese invaders, MacArthur issued these statements from Australia on April 10, and May 7, 1942.

The Bataan Force went out as it would have wished, fighting to the end its flickering forlorn hope. No army has ever done so much with so little and nothing became it more than its last hour of trial and agony. To the weeping Mothers of its dead, I can only say that the sacrifice and halo of Jesus of Nazareth has descended upon their sons, and that God will take them unto himself.

Corregidor needs no comment from me. It has sounded its own story at the mouth of its guns. It has scrolled its own epitaph on enemy tablets. But through the bloody haze of its last reverberating shot, I shall always seem to see a vision of grim, gaunt, ghastly men, still unafraid.

[1] Reprinted by permission of the Bureau of Archives, MacArthur Memorial.

6
Return to the Philippines (1944)[1]

MacArthur had vowed to return to the Philippines to liberate the islands from the Japanese, and he achieved his wish on October 17, 1944, when his troops landed at Leyte Beach. With the beachhead barely secured, he waded into shore and delivered this message into a waiting microphone.

People of the Philippines: I have returned. By the grace of Almighty God our forces stand again on Philippine soil—soil consecrated in the blood of our two peoples. We have come, dedicated and committed, to the task of destroying every vestige of enemy control over your daily lives, and of restoring, upon a foundation of indestructible strength, the liberties of your people.

At my side is your President, Sergio Osmena, worthy successor to that great patriot, Manuel Quezon, with members of his cabinet. The seat of your government is now therefore firmly re-established on Philippine soil.

The hour of your redemption is here. Your patriots have demonstrated an unswerving and resolute devotion to the principles of freedom that challenges the best that is written on the pages of human history. I now call upon your supreme effort that the enemy may know from the temper of an aroused and outraged people within that he has a force there to contend with no less violent than is the force committed from without.

Rally to me. Let the indomitable spirit of Bataan and Corregidor lead on. As the lines of battle roll forward to bring you within the zone of operations, rise and strike. Strike at every favorable opportunity. For your home and hearths, strike! For future generations of your sons and daughters, strike! In the name of your sacred dead, strike! Let no heart be faint. Let every arm be steeled. The guidance of divine God points the way. Follow in His Name to the Holy Grail of righteous victory.

[1] Reprinted by permission of the Bureau of Archives, MacArthur Memorial.

7
The Japanese Surrender
(1945)[1]

MacArthur formally received the Japanese surrender on board the battleship Missouri *in Tokyo Bay on September 2, 1945. After the ceremonies, he delivered this address to the American people.*

Today the guns are silent. A great tragedy has ended. A great victory has been won. The skies no longer rain death—the seas bear only commerce—men everywhere walk upright in the sunlight. The entire world lies quietly at peace. The holy mission has been completed. And in reporting this to you, the people, I speak for the thousands of silent lips, forever stilled among the jungles and the beaches and in the deep waters of the Pacific which marked the way. I speak for the unnamed brave millions homeward bound to take up the challenge of that future which they did so much to salvage from the brink of disaster.

As I look back on the long, tortuous trail from those grim days of Bataan and Corregidor, when an entire world lived in fear, when democracy was on the defensive everywhere, when modern civilization trembled in the balance, I thank a merciful God that he has given us the faith, the courage, and the power from which to mould victory. We have known the bitterness of defeat and the exultation of triumph, and from both we have learned there can be no turning back. We must go forward to preserve in peace what we won in war.

A new era is upon us. Even the lesson of victory itself brings with it profound concern, both for our future security and the survival of civilization. The destructiveness of the war potential, through progressive advances in scientific discovery, has in fact now reached a point which revises the traditional concept of war.

Men since the beginning of time have sought peace. Various methods through the ages have been attempted to devise an international process to prevent or settle disputes between nations. From the very start workable methods were found in so far as individual citizens were

[1] Reprinted by permission of the Bureau of Archives, MacArthur Memorial.

concerned, but the mechanics of an instrumentality of larger international scope have never been successful. Military alliances, balance of power, Leagues of Nations all in turn failed, leaving the only path to be by way of the crucible of war. The utter destructiveness of war now blots out this alternative. We have had our last chance. If we do not devise some greater and more equitable system Armageddon will be at our door. The problem basically is theological and involves a spiritual recrudescence and improvement of human character that will synchronize with our almost matchless advance in science, art, literature, and all material and cultural developments of the past two thousand years. It must be of the spirit if we are to save the flesh.

We stand in Tokyo today reminiscent of our countryman Commodore Perry ninety-two years ago. His purpose was to bring to Japan an era of enlightenment and progress by lifting the veil of isolation to the friendship, trade, and commerce of the world. But alas the knowledge thereby gained of Western science was forged into an instrument of oppression and human enslavement. Freedom of expression, freedom of action, even freedom of thought were denied through suppression of liberal education, through appeal to superstition, and through the application of force. We are committed by the Potsdam Declaration of Principles to see that the Japanese people are liberated from this condition of slavery. It is my purpose to implement this commitment just as rapidly as the armed forces are demobilized and other essential steps taken to neutralize the war potential. The energy of the Japanese race, if properly directed, will enable expansion vertically rather than horizontally. If the talents of the race are turned into constructive channels, the country can lift itself from its present deplorable state into a position of dignity.

To the Pacific basin has come the vista of a new emancipated world. Today, freedom is on the offensive, democracy is on the march. Today, in Asia as well as in Europe, unshackled peoples are tasting the full sweetness of liberty, the relief from fear.

In the Philippines, America has evolved a model for this new free world of Asia. In the Philippines, America has demonstrated that peoples of the East and peoples of the West may walk side by side in mutual respect and with mutual benefit. The history of our sovereignty there has now the full confidence of the East.

And so, my fellow countrymen, today I report to you that your sons and daughters have served you well and faithfully with the calm, deliberate, determined fighting spirit of the American soldier and sailor based upon a tradition of historical truth, as against the fanaticism of an enemy supported only by mythological fiction. Their spiritual strength and power has brought us through to victory. They are homeward bound—take care of them.

8
The Occupation of Japan (1947)[1]

On September 2, 1947, MacArthur issued this report on the progress of the American Occupation of Japan.

Two years have now passed since that fateful September 2nd on the *Missouri,* when the Allies on the one hand and the Japanese on the other entered into the solemn commitments underlying surrender conditions. It is unnecessary to restate the results of the ensuing occupation as they are now largely of historical record, but it is appropriate today to reflect upon the lesson learned, not alone in terms of the present and the immediate future, but more particularly its long-range influence upon the progress of civilization. For the opportunity here afforded to bring to a race, long stunted by ancient concepts of mythological teaching, the refreshing uplift of enlightenment and truth and reality, with practical demonstrations of Christian ideals, is of deep and universal significance.

During those two years, both sides—Allies and Japanese—have by adherence to the letter and spirit of their respective undertakings acquitted themselves honorably and well—and both have benefited from the relationship. History records no other instance wherein the military occupation of a conquered people has been conducted with the emphasis placed, as it has been here, upon the moral values involved between victor and vanquished. Right rather than might has been the criterion. The fruits of this policy are now self-evident. Japan today stands out as one of the few places in a distraught world where, despite an economy of critically short supply, there is a minimum of fear, of confusion, and of unrest—where the people are diligently endeavoring to expiate the breach of the peace for which their nation stands universally condemned, to overcome the poverty left by war and defeat, and to elevate themselves to trusted and useful membership in the family of nations. Avoiding vengeance, intolerance, and injustice, Allied policy, apart from its rigidly destructive phase designed to eliminate from Japanese life both the will and the capacity to wage war, has rested squarely upon the fundamental concept which

[1] Reprinted by permission of the Bureau of Archives, MacArthur Memorial.

finds immortal exposition in the Sermon on the Mount. And by bringing into clear focus the commanding influence moral values thus have played in this relationship between nations and men, the results here attained invoke standards which might well be recognized and carried forward if the grave international issues which perplex mankind are to be resolved dispassionately in harmony and peace. There is no novelty in this simple concept, but too often it is ignored in the international sphere—betrayed through the misuse of power over the lives and destinies of others, with war the price the world inevitably has paid for this, man's greatest folly.

A peace treaty is shortly to be discussed. It is essential that it be approached in that some tolerant and just atmosphere to insure that this defeated country has the opportunity to become self-sustaining, rather than reduced to a condition of mendicancy. A post-treaty Japan should not become a burden upon the economy of any other country. For it is a well-tested historical truism that a people given a fair chance will reach the niche in human society to which their own industry, their own skill, and their own perseverance entitle them, without largess from others—that largess stultifies rather than quickens private initiative and individual energy, so essential to human progress. It is furthermore a false concept which contends that democracy can only thrive if maintained in plenty. On the contrary, history shows that it springs from hardship and struggle and toil, to flourish naturally in the hearts of men who cherish individual freedom and dignity—or not at all. A spiritual commodity, it is neither for purchase nor for sale.

There need be no concern over fears recently expressed of imminent economic collapse. It must be understood that the actual collapse of the Japanese economy, which was a major Allied war aim, occurred prior to the surrender as a result of attrition caused by the crushing force of Allied arms, the severance of Japan's lifelines abroad, the wresting from Japan of Manchuria, Korea, Formosa and the island groups mandated to her following the First World War, and the destruction of Japan's shipping afloat and her centers of industry and commerce at home. The economic prostration of the country was complete at the beginning of the occupation, industry then being at a practical standstill. In reality, since the surrender, under the guidance of the occupation and with American help, Japan has been gradually restoring her shattered economy and the curve is up not down. The industrial output has now risen to over 45 per cent of pre-war normal, and the improvement can be expected to continue. This relative stability, especially by comparison with more fortunately favored countries, and even under the blighting effects of practical blockade, has been one of the most amazing and encouraging features of the occupation period. To become self-supporting, however, it is essential that the economic isolation imposed by the Allies be modified so that trade with the outside world can be resumed.

If Japan in the post-treaty era is given a just opportunity to live in freedom and peace with her neighbors in the community of nations, there will be no threat to the survival and strengthening of the democratic processes here inaugurated under the occupation. For democracy, once firmly rooted in the human heart, has never voluntarily yielded before any other conflicting ideology known to man. If liberty and public morality do not bring national stability, nothing can.

9

MacArthur Praises American Traditions (1947)[1]

Throughout his career, MacArthur was lavishly praised by the ultra-conservative Hearst press. This letter from MacArthur illustrates a number of their areas of agreement.

Unlike the historical background of many other nations and peoples, our country finds its roots firmly planted in the great and immutable concepts of human freedom and individual dignity. Evolution, as men have groped for more understanding with civilization's advance and as populations have increased and scientific and technological knowledge progressed, has failed to dim the luster of these concepts or to show them to be in any respect outmoded. As they served to guide the architects to our free way of life and the decisions of countless American leaders through the generations which since have passed, so now these same basic concepts yet stand as the sturdy foundation upon which rests, and must always rest, our strength as a nation and our progress as a people.

Only in the present generation has persuasion been offered to reshape our lives and institutions away from these concepts. Only in recent years has the demand been made that our course, long firmly charted along the path of a free and plentiful life, be radically altered to embrace new concepts and new ideas, all premised upon novel and yet untested ideological variations. Only in contemporary life have we found ourselves pressed, as we search for the solution to the problems and issues of the present, to ignore the challenging lessons of history and experience and human progress and to disdain the counsel of American leadership which carried us safely through many turbulent years of the past.

The results attained along this altered course of public thinking and public planning and public action have in many respects not been contributive to the well-being of our people, nor to the strengthening of our free way of life. For our country, however large and powerful it has become, has by no means outgrown those same simple

---

[1] From Douglas MacArthur to John R. Hearst, October 27, 1947. Reprinted by permission of the Bureau of Archives, MacArthur Memorial.

concepts which through successive generations have formed the cornerstone to our free institutions, on which we have placed implicit reliance—and justifiably so—in the recurrent crises of war and peace.

It is thus quite clear that in that great pattern of unparalleled human progress which we ourselves have given to civilization—in that basic dogma which has provided us with personal liberty and individual dignity and encouraged the maximum of human productivity through our traditional system of free private competitive enterprise, alone capable of maximizing human initiative and energy—and in the lessons of history revealing the calm judgment of our forefathers in their approach to the no less complex problems of their time, lie the norms and guides to the solution of most of the vexatious issues which appear to harass us in ours.

10
Formosa Is Vital to
United States Security (1950)[1]

By 1950, MacArthur had emerged as one of the keenest supporters of the faltering Nationalist regime in Formosa. In July, shortly after the outbreak of the Korean War, MacArthur flew to Formosa for an extremely cordial visit with Generalissimo and Madame Chiang Kai-shek, after which Chiang issued a statement speaking of "Sino-American military cooperation." President Truman, under pressure from America's military allies, sought to cool MacArthur's public ardor for Chiang's discredited regime, but to no avail. MacArthur sent this message to a Chicago convention of the Veterans of Foreign Wars to be held on August 27, 1950. When Truman heard of it, he ordered it withdrawn, but his order arrived too late to prevent publication.

In view of misconceptions currently being voiced concerning the relationship of Formosa to our strategic potential in the Pacific, I believe it in the public interest to avail myself of this opportunity to state my views thereon to you, all of whom having fought overseas understand broad strategic concepts. To begin with, any appraisal of that strategic potential requires an appreciation of the changes wrought in the course of the past war. Prior thereto the Western strategic frontier of the United States lay on the littoral line of the Americas with an exposed island salient extending out through Hawaii, Midway and Guam to the Philippines. That salient was not an outpost of strength but an avenue of weakness along which the enemy could and did attack us. The Pacific was a potential area of advance for any predatory force intent upon striking at the bordering land areas.

All of this was changed by our Pacific victory. Our strategic frontier then shifted to embrace the entire Pacific Ocean, which has become a vast moat to protect us as long as we hold it. Indeed, it acts as a protective shield for all of the Americas and all free lands of the Pacific Ocean area. We control it to the shores of Asia by a chain of islands extending in an arc from the Aleutians to the Mariannas held by us and our free allies. From this island chain we can dominate with air power every Asiatic port from Vladivostok to Singapore and pre-

[1] Reprinted by permission of the Bureau of Archives, MacArthur Memorial.

vent any hostile movement into the Pacific. Any predatory attack from Asia must be an amphibious effort. No amphibious force can be successful without control of the sea lanes and the air over these lanes in its avenue of advance. With naval and air supremacy and modest ground elements to defend bases, any major attack from continental Asia toward us or our friends of the Pacific would be doomed to failure. Under such conditions the Pacific no longer represents menacing avenues of approach for a prospective invader—it assumes instead the friendly aspect of a peaceful lake. Our line of defense is a natural one and can be maintained with a minimum of military effort and expense. It envisions no attack against anyone nor does it provide the bastions essential for offensive operations, but properly maintained would be an invincible defense against aggression. If we hold this line we may have peace—lose it and war is inevitable.

The geographic location of Formosa is such that in the hands of a power unfriendly to the United States it constitutes an enemy salient in the very center of this defensive perimeter, 100–150 miles closer to the adjacent friendly segments—Okinawa and the Philippines—than any point in continental Asia. At the present time there is on Formosa a concentration of operational air and naval bases which is potentially greater than any similar concentration on the Asiatic mainland between the Yellow Sea and the Strait of Malacca. Additional bases can be developed in a relatively short time by an aggressive exploitation of all World War II Japanese facilities. An enemy force utilizing those installations currently available could increase by 100 per cent the air effort which could be directed against Okinawa as compared to operations based on the mainland and at the same time could direct damaging air attacks with fighter-type aircraft against friendly installations in the Philippines which are currently beyond the range of fighters based on the mainland. Our air supremacy at once would become doubtful.

As a result of its geographical location and base potential, utilization of Formosa by a military power hostile to the United States may either counterbalance or overshadow the strategic importance of the central and southern flank of the United States front-line position. Formosa in the hands of such a hostile power could be compared to an unsinkable aircraft carrier and submarine tender ideally located to accomplish offensive strategy and at the same time checkmate defensive or counter-offensive operations by friendly forces based on Okinawa and the Philippines. This unsinkable carrier-tender has the capacity to operate from ten to twenty air groups of types ranging from jet fighters to B-29-type bombers, as well as to provide forward operating facilities for short-range coastal submarines. In acquiring this forward submarine base, the efficacy of the short-range submarine would be so enormously increased by the addition radius of activity as to threaten completely sea traffic from the south and interdict all sea lanes in the Western Pacific. Submarine blockade by the enemy with all its destructive ramifications would thereby become a virtual certainty.

Should Formosa fall and bases thereafter come into the hands of a potential enemy of the United States, the latter will have acquired an additional "fleet" which will have been obtained and can be maintained at an incomparably lower cost than could its equivalent in aircraft carriers and submarine tenders. Current estimates of air and submarine resources in the Far East indicate the capability of such a potential enemy to extend his forces southward and still maintain an imposing degree of military strength for employment elsewhere in the Pacific area.

Historically, Formosa has been used as a springboard for just such military aggression directed against areas to the south. The most notable and recent example was the utilization of it by the Japanese in World War II. At the outbreak of the Pacific War in 1941, it played an important part as a staging area and supporting base for the various Japanese invasion convoys. The supporting air forces of Japan's army and navy were based on fields situated along southern Formosa. From 1942 through 1944, Formosa was a vital link in the transportation and communications chain which stretched from Japan through Okinawa and the Philippines to Southeast Asia. As the United States carrier forces advanced into the Western Pacific, the bases on Formosa assumed an increasingly greater role in the Japanese defense scheme. Should Formosa fall in the hands of a hostile power, history would repeat itself. Its military potential would again be fully exploited as the means to breach and neutralize our Western Pacific defense system and mount a war of conquest against the free nations of the Pacific Basin.

Nothing could be more fallacious than the threadbare argument by those who advocate appeasement and defeatism in the Pacific that if we defend Formosa we alienate continental Asia. Those who speak thus do not understand the Orient. They do not grasp that it is in the pattern of Oriental psychology to respect and follow aggressive, resolute and dynamic leadership—to quickly turn from a leadership characterized by timidity or vacillation—and they underestimate the Oriental mentality. Nothing in the last five years has so inspired the Far East as the American determination to preserve the bulwarks of our Pacific Ocean strategic position from future encroachment, for few of its peoples fail accurately to appraise the safeguard such determination brings to their free institutions. To pursue any other course would be to turn over the fruits of our Pacific victory to a potential enemy. It would shift any future battle area 5,000 miles eastward to the coasts of the American continents, our own home coasts; it would completely expose our friends in the Philippines, our friends in Australia and New Zealand, our friends in Indonesia, our friends in Japan, and other areas to the lustful thrusts of those who stand for slavery as against liberty, for atheism as against God.

The decision of President Truman on June 27th lighted into flame a lamp of hope throughout Asia that was burning dimly towards extinction. It marked for the Far East the focal and turning point in this area's struggle for freedom. It swept aside in one great monumental stroke all of the hypocrisy and the sophistry which has confused and deluded so many people distant from the actual scene.

11

Telegram to Congressman
Joseph Martin (1951)[1]

*On March 8, the House Minority Leader, Congress-
man Joseph Martin of Massachusetts, wrote to MacArthur and
enclosed a speech in which he urged that "the forces of Generalissimo Chiang Kai-shek on Formosa . . . be employed in the
opening of a second Asiatic front." He requested MacArthur's
views on this subject. On March 20, MacArthur replied in a
famous letter which Martin later read on the floor of the House
of Representatives.*

March 20, 1951

Dear Congressman Martin: I am most grateful for your note of
the 8th forwarding me a copy of your address of February 12. The
latter I have read with much interest and find that with the passage
of years you have certainly lost none of your old-time punch.

My views and recommendations with respect to the situation created
by Red China's entry into war against us in Korea have been submitted to Washington in most complete detail. Generally these views
are well known and clearly understood, as they follow the conventional
pattern of meeting force with maximum counter force as we have
never failed to do in the past. Your view with respect to the utilization of the Chinese forces on Formosa is in conflict with neither logic
nor this tradition.

It seems strangely difficult for some to realize that here in Asia is
where the Communist conspirators have elected to make their play
for global conquest, and that we have joined the issue thus raised on
the battlefield; that here we fight Europe's war with arms while the
diplomats there still fight it with words; that if we lose the war to
communism in Asia the fall of Europe is inevitable, win it and Europe
most probably would avoid war and yet preserve freedom. As you
point out we must win. There is no substitute for victory.

With renewed thanks and expressions of most cordial regard, I am

Faithfully yours,

Douglas MacArthur

---

[1] From U.S. House of Representatives, 82nd Cong., 1st sess., *Congressional Record*,
97, Part 3 (April 5, 1951): 3380.

45

12

Old Soldiers Never Die (1951)[1]

Relieved of his commands by President Truman, Mac-Arthur returned to a tumultuous reception in the United States. Invited to address a joint meeting of Congress, MacArthur availed himself of this opportunity to publicize his views on foreign policy by delivering this speech on April 19, 1951. It is probably the most widely known and frequently quoted of all his public statements.

Mr. President, Mr. Speaker, and distinguished Members of the Congress, I stand on this rostrum with a sense of deep humility and great pride—humility in the wake of those great American architects of our history who have stood here before me, pride in the reflection that this forum of legislative debate represents human liberty in the purest form yet devised. [Applause.] Here are centered the hopes, and aspirations, and faith of the entire human race.

I do not stand here as advocate for any partisan cause, for the issues are fundamental and reach quite beyond the realm of partisan consideration. They must be resolved on the highest plane of national interest if our course is to prove sound and our future protected. I trust, therefore, that you will do me the justice of receiving that which I have to say as solely expressing the considered viewpoint of a fellow American. I address you with neither rancor nor bitterness in the fading twilight of life with but one purpose in mind—to serve my country. [Applause.]

The issues are global and so interlocked that to consider the problems of one sector, oblivious to those of another, is but to court disaster for the whole.

While Asia is commonly referred to as the gateway to Europe, it is no less true that Europe is the gateway to Asia, and the broad influence of the one cannot fail to have its impact upon the other.

There are those who claim our strength is inadequate to protect on both fronts—that we cannot divide our effort. I can think of no greater expression of defeatism. [Applause.] If a potential enemy can divide his strength on two fronts, it is for us to counter his effort.

---

[1] From U.S. House of Representatives, 82nd Cong., 1st sess., *Congressional Record*, 97, Part 3 (April 19, 1951): 4123–25.

The Communist threat is a global one. Its successful advance in one sector threatens the destruction of every other sector. You cannot appease or otherwise surrender to communism in Asia without simultaneously undermining our efforts to halt its advance in Europe. [Applause.]

Beyond pointing out these general truisms, I shall confine my discussion to the general areas of Asia. Before one may objectively assess the situation now existing there, he must comprehend something of Asia's past and the revolutionary changes which have marked her course up to the present. Long exploited by the so-called colonial powers, with little opportunity to achieve any degree of social justice, individual dignity, or a higher standard of life such as guided our own noble administration of the Philippines, the peoples of Asia found their opportunity in the war just past to throw off the shackles of colonialism, and now see the dawn of new opportunity, a heretofore unfelt dignity and the self-respect of political freedom.

Mustering half of the earth's population and 60 percent of its natural resources, these peoples are rapidly consolidating a new force, both moral and material, with which to raise the living standard and erect adaptations of the design of modern progress to their own distinct cultural environments. Whether one adheres to the concept of colonization or not, this is the direction of Asian progress and it may not be stopped. It is a corollary to the shift of the world economic frontiers, as the whole epicenter of world affairs rotates back toward the area whence it started. . . .

To understand the changes which now appear upon the Chinese mainland, one must understand the changes in Chinese character and culture over the past 50 years. China up to 50 years ago was completely nonhomogeneous, being compartmented into groups divided against each other. The war-making tendency was almost nonexistent, as they still followed the tenets of the Confucian ideal of pacifist culture. At the turn of the century, under the regime of Chan So Lin, efforts toward greater homogeneity produced the start of a nationalist urge. This was further and more successfully developed under the leadership of Chiang Kai-shek, but has been brought to its greatest fruition under the present regime, to the point that it has now taken on the character of a united nationalism of increasingly dominant aggressive tendencies. Through these past 50 years, the Chinese people have thus become militarized in their concepts and in their ideals. They now constitute excellent soldiers with competent staffs and commanders. This has produced a new and dominant power in Asia which for its own purposes is allied with Soviet Russia, but which in its own concepts and methods has become aggressively imperialistic with a lust for expansion and increased power normal to this type of imperialism. There is little of the ideological concept either one way or another in the Chinese make-up. The standard of living is so low and the capital accumulation has been so thoroughly dissipated by war that the masses are desperate and avid to follow any leadership which seems to promise the alleviation of local stringencies. I have from the beginning believed that the Chinese Communists' support of the North Koreans was the dominant one. Their interests are at present parallel to those of the Soviet, but I believe that the aggressiveness recently displayed not only in Korea, but also in Indochina and Tibet and pointing potentially toward the south, reflects predominantly the same lust for the expansion of power which has animated every would-be conqueror since the beginning of time. [Applause.]

The Japanese people since the war have undergone the greatest reformation recorded in modern history. With a commendable will, eagerness to learn, and marked capacity to understand, they have, from the ashes left in war's wake, erected in Japan an edifice dedicated to the primacy of individual liberty and personal dignity, and in the ensuing process there has been created a truly representative government committed to the advance of political morality, freedom of economic enterprise and social justice. [Applause.] Politically, economically and socially Japan is now abreast of many free nations of the earth and will not again fail the universal trust. That it may be counted upon to wield a profoundly beneficial influence over the course of events in Asia is attested by the magnificent manner in which the Japanese people have met the recent challenge of war, unrest, and confusion surrounding them from the outside, and checked communism within their own frontiers without the slightest slackening in their forward progress. I sent all four of our occupation divisions to the Korean battle front without the slightest qualms as to the effect of the resulting power vacuum upon Japan. The results fully justified my faith. [Applause.] I know of no nation more serene, orderly, and industrious—nor in which higher hopes can be entertained for future constructive service in the advance of the human race. [Applause.]

Of our former wards, the Philippines, we can look forward in confidence that the existing unrest will be corrected and a strong and healthy nation will grow in the longer aftermath of war's terrible destructiveness. We must be patient and understanding and never fail them, as in our hour of need they did not fail us. [Applause.] A Christian nation, the Philippines stand as a mighty bulwark of Christianity in the Far East, and its capacity for high moral leadership in Asia is unlimited.

On Formosa, the Government of the Republic of China has had the opportunity to refute by action much of the malicious gossip which so undermined the strength of its leadership on the Chinese mainland. [Applause.] The Formosan people are receiving a just and enlightened administration with majority representation on the organs of government; and politically, economically and socially they appear to be advancing along sound and constructive lines.

With this brief insight into the surrounding areas I now turn to the Korean conflict. While I was not consulted prior to the President's decision to intervene in support of the Republic of Korea, that decision, from a military standpoint, proved a sound one [applause] as we hurled back the invaders and decimated his forces. Our victory was complete and our objectives within reach when Red China intervened with numerically superior ground forces. This created a new war and an entirely new situation—a situation not contemplated when our forces were committed against the North Korean invaders—a situation which called for new decisions in the diplomatic sphere to permit the realistic adjustment of military strategy. Such decisions have not been forthcoming. [Applause.]

While no man in his right mind would advocate sending our ground forces into continental China and such was never given a thought, the new situation did urgently demand a drastic revision of strategic planning if our political aim was to defeat this new enemy as we had defeated the old. [Applause.]

Apart from the military need as I saw it to neutralize the sanctuary protection given the enemy north of the Yalu, I felt that military necessity in the conduct of the war made mandatory:

1. The intensification of our economic blockade against China;
2. The imposition of a naval blockade against the China coast;
3. Removal of restrictions on air reconnaissance of China's coast areas and of Manchuria [applause];
4. Removal of restrictions on the forces of the Republic of China on Formosa with logistical support to contribute to their effective operations against the common enemy. [Applause.]

For entertaining these views, all professionally designed to support our forces committed to Korea and bring hostilities to an end with the least possible delay and at a saving of countless American and

Allied lives, I have been severely criticized in lay circles, principally abroad, despite my understanding that from a military standpoint the above views have been fully shared in the past by practically every military leader concerned with the Korean campaign, including our own Joint Chiefs of Staff. [Applause, the Members rising.]

I called for reinforcements, but was informed that reinforcements were not available. I made clear that if not permitted to destroy the build-up bases north of the Yalu; if not permitted to utilize the friendly Chinese force of some 600,000 men on Formosa; if not permitted to blockade the China coast to prevent the Chinese Reds from getting succor from without; and if there were to be no hope of major reinforcements, the position of the command from the military standpoint forbade victory. We could hold in Korea by constant maneuver and at an approximate area where our supply line advantages were in balance with the supply line disadvantages of the enemy, but we could hope at best for only an indecisive campaign, with its terrible and constant attrition upon our forces if the enemy utilized his full military potential. I have constantly called for the new political decisions essential to a solution. Efforts have been made to distort my position. It has been said, in effect, that I am a warmonger. Nothing could be further from the truth. I know war as few other men now living know it, and nothing to me is more revolting. I have long advocated its complete abolition as its very destructiveness on both friend and foe has rendered it useless as a means of settling international disputes. . . .

But once war is forced upon us, there is no other alternative than to apply every available means to bring it to a swift end. War's very object is victory—not prolonged indecision. [Applause.] In war, indeed, there can be no substitute for victory. [Applause.]

There are some who for varying reasons would appease Red China. They are blind to history's clear lesson. For history teaches with unmistakable emphasis that appeasement but begets new and bloodier war. It points to no single instance where the end has justified that means—where appeasement has led to more than a sham peace. Like blackmail, it lays the basis for new and successively greater demands, until, as in blackmail, violence becomes the only other alternative. Why, my soldiers asked of me, surrender military advantages to an enemy in the field? I could not answer. [Applause.] Some may say to avoid spread of the conflict into an all-out war with China; others, to avoid Soviet intervention. Neither explanation seems valid. For China is already engaging with the maximum power it can commit and the

Soviet will not necessarily mesh its actions with our moves. Like a cobra, any new enemy will more likely strike whenever it feels that the relativity in military or other potential is in its favor on a world-wide basis.

The tragedy of Korea is further heightened by the fact that as military action is confined to its territorial limits, it condemns that nation, which it is our purpose to save, to suffer the devastating impact of full naval and air bombardment, while the enemy's sanctuaries are fully protected from such attack and devastation. Of the nations of the world, Korea alone, up to now, is the sole one which has risked its all against communism. The magnificence of the courage and fortitude of the Korean people defies description. [Applause.] They have chosen to risk death rather than slavery. Their last words to me were "Don't scuttle the Pacific." [Applause.]

I have just left your fighting sons in Korea. They have met all tests there and I can report to you without reservation they are splendid in every way. [Applause.] It was my constant effort to preserve them and end this savage conflict honorably and with the least loss of time and a minimum sacrifice of life. Its growing bloodshed has caused me the deepest anguish and anxiety. Those gallant men will remain often in my thoughts and in my prayers always. [Applause.]

I am closing my 52 years of military service. [Applause.] When I joined the Army even before the turn of the century, it was the fulfillment of all my boyish hopes and dreams. The world has turned over many times since I took the oath on the plain at West Point, and the hopes and dreams have long since vanished. But I still remember the refrain of one of the most popular barrack ballads of that day which proclaimed most proudly that—

"Old soldiers never die; they just fade away."

And like the old soldier of that ballad, I now close my military career and just fade away—an old soldier who tried to do his duty as God gave him the light to see that duty.

Good-by.

13

The Conduct of the Korean War (1951)[1]

From May 3 to June 25, 1951, the Senate Armed Services Committee and the Senate Foreign Relations Committee held joint hearings on American policy in the Far East. MacArthur was the star witness. Eventually, the hearings proved to be exhausting and inconclusive, with over 2,045,000 words of testimony. These are two of the more striking excerpts.

Senator Green. What I would like to ask is a question which seems to me to go to the basis of the whole difference that has been developed. It is this:

The theory that we could win a quick victory in China simply by lending logistic support to the Chinese troops now in Formosa and in bombarding the coast cities and in establishing blockage would, in the first place, would it not, indicate we would proceed alone and not with any help from the other United Nations?

General MacArthur. I can give you no testimony about the United Nations, Senator.

Senator Green. What would be your expectation?

General MacArthur. My hope would be of course that the United Nations would see the wisdom and utility of that course, but if they did not, I still believe that the interest of the United States being the predominant one in Korea, would require our action.

Senator Green. Alone?

General MacArthur. Alone, if necessary. If the other nations of the world haven't got enough sense to see where appeasement leads after the appeasement which led to the Second World War in Europe, if they can't see exactly the road that they are following in Asia, why then we had better protect ourselves and go it alone.

Senator Green. Then why do you think that the Chinese now in Formosa, even with that help and without our ground forces in China, could achieve a victory when Chiang Kai-shek suffered such a severe defeat previously?

[1] U.S. Senate, Committee on Armed Services and the Committee on Foreign Relations, *Military Situation in the Far East,* 82nd Cong., 1st sess. (May, 1951): 42, 68.

General MacArthur. I don't believe that the Chinese Nationalist forces alone, Senator, could achieve any such victory, but using them in conjunction with our own forces in accordance with the recommendations the Joint Chiefs of Staff made January 12, I believe that we would achieve a victory within a reasonable period of time.

I believe that the Chinese, the potential of China to wage modern war, is limited. She lacks the industrial base upon which modern war is based. . . .

General MacArthur. Now, war never before in the history of the world has been applied in a piecemeal way, that you make half war, and not whole war.

Now, that China is using the maximum of her force against us is quite evident; and we are not using the maximum of ours against her, in reply.

The result is—we do not even use, to the maximum, the forces at our disposal, the scientific methods, and the result is that for every percentage you take away in the use of the Air and the Navy, you add a percentage to the dead American infantrymen.

It may seem emotional for me to say that, but I happen to be the man that had to send them into it. The blood, to some extent, would rest on me; and with the objectives, I believe I could stop them—it seems terrific to me that we should not attempt something.

The inertia that exists. There is no policy—there is nothing, I tell you, no plan, or anything.

When you say, merely, "we are going to continue to fight aggression," that is not what the enemy is fighting for.

The enemy is fighting for a very definite purpose—to destroy our forces in Korea.

We constantly, every day, run that risk, without the potential of defeating him, and stopping him—to come again.

He attacks today. We resist it. We fall back. We form a new line, and we surge back.

Then, he is right back, within a week, maybe, up to the battle front with his inexhaustible supply of manpower. He brings in another hundred thousand, or another half-million men, and tosses them at these troops constantly.

That is a new concept in war.

That is not war—that is appeasement.

14

A Defense of American Capitalism (1952)[1]

On December 5, 1952, four months after becoming the Chairman of the Board of the Remington Rand Corporation, MacArthur made this speech to the 57th Congress of American Industry, sponsored by the National Association of Manufacturers, in New York City's Waldorf-Astoria Hotel.

The past twenty years have witnessed an incessant encroachment upon the capitalistic system through the direction of our own policy. This has left our free economy badly bruised and sorely tried. The assault has taken various forms. For political expediency and even baser purposes, efforts have constantly been made by those in power or those seeking to be in power to provoke distrust and strife between industrial owners and industrial workers, between management and labor—to breech the community of purpose and effort which so logically must exist between these two great segments of our industrial economy. The effect of this has been to produce a sense of unrest and antagonism where a firm and confident alliance built upon a mutuality of faith and understanding and a community of purpose will not only serve the interests of both, but further the well-being of that third great economic segment, the consuming public.

Another and yet more serious form of assault upon the capitalistic system has been the increasingly oppressive government levies upon both capital and profit. The principle underlying such levies has not been to equalize the burden of meeting the legitimate costs of government by a just and uniform assessment, but has followed instead a conspiratorial design originally evolved by Karl Marx to first weaken and then destroy the capitalistic system. Thus, many of our tax laws amount in practical effect to a series of graduated penalties upon the efficiency and the thrift which produces profit and accumulates capital —penalties which strike at the very roots of the incentive to labor, to create and to cheerfully accept the risks and hazards of enterprise in the traditional American pioneering spirit.

Karl Marx shunned the use of violence and sought the voluntary

[1] Reprinted by permission of the Bureau of Archives, MacArthur Memorial.

54

acceptance of the principle of communal ownership of the sources and means of production. The innate common sense of the human race, however, rejected this principle and the element of force was injected by the Bolsheviks after the close of the First World War. Then was combined the theory of Karl Marx with the principle of Nihilism under which the control of public policy was sought through terrorism and assassination. This combination known as Communism was far more successful. The minority in many sectors of the globe was able to establish its rule over the majority. Only where the concept of human liberty was most deeply rooted and greatly advanced were such minority pressures decisively thrown back.

Such was the case in this nation where our economy, built upon the principle of private capitalism, became recognized as the great barrier to the universal enforcement of the theories of modern Communism. There followed repeated and diversified efforts to reduce and destroy it. Resort was had to the control of private profit by the Marxism-inspired device of confiscatory taxation and the absorption of private wealth by inheritance, gift and other direct levies upon privately accumulated resources. Most officials of our government over the past years will deny, and justifiably, any intent to establish in this nation the basis for the emergence of a Socialistic or even eventually a Communistic state, but the course of fiscal policy has done just that.

The fact is unmistakable and clear that if the capitalistic system— free enterprise—is to be preserved to the future generations of our people, the course of government must now be sharply reoriented and America's industrial leadership must assume an invincible and uncompromising defense of that system. Only thereby may there be fostered and preserved adequate incentive to encourage the thrift, the industry and the adventure which brought our nation to its present preeminence among all of the other nations of the earth and which alone can carry it forward in peace and security and progress.

In accordance with our constitutional precepts, we are now about to send a new administration to Washington to assume the reins of government. It is an administration chosen by the American people in reliance upon the pledge that in domestic affairs it will root out corruption, waste, incompetence and subversion in the public administration; that it will sharply reduce the costs of government and lighten the existing burdens of taxation; that it will abolish unnecessary control by government upon business and otherwise curb unjustifiable interference by government in private affairs; that it will stem the spiral of inflation and through sound fiscal policy gradually restore the lost purchasing value of the dollar; and that it will stop the advance of Socialism in this country and re-establish measures designed to encourage the development of our traditional free enterprise economy.

This pledge accepted by mandate of the electorate is deserving of the full faith of America's industrial leadership. For under our system of government and in the American tradition, it becomes our duty as citizens to rally in firm support of the new administration and give it every chance and assistance within individual and collective power to fulfill its pledge and restore to the country a prosperity based upon sound rather than illusory considerations.

We must not fear the return to this land of normalcy merely because of the possible temporary dislocation of our economy now so largely resting upon the production in massive quantities of the sinews of war. We must not fear to end the reckless and exhausting extravagance of government merely because it may force upon us an increase of frugality. Better if need be we increase our own thrift than leave our children and children's children a heritage of want and despair.

15

The Secret Plan to
End the War (1954)[1]

Shortly after MacArthur's death, Bob Considine of the Hearst Press published the substance of an interview he had had with the general on January 27, 1954. According to Considine, MacArthur had "died embittered" by the knowledge that his advice on the Korean War had been rejected not only by President Truman, but by his former aide, Dwight D. Eisenhower. In this selection from that interview, MacArthur discussed his secret plan to end the war.

Of all the campaigns of my life, 20 major ones to be exact, the one I felt most sure of was the one I was deprived of waging. I could have won the war in Korea in a maximum of 10 days, with considerably fewer casualties than were suffered during the so-called truce period, and it would have altered the course of history.

The enemy's air (power) would first have been taken out. I would have dropped between 30 and 50 atomic bombs on his air bases and other depots strung across the neck of Manchuria from just across the Yalu River from Antung (northwestern tip of Korea) to the neighborhood of Hunchun (just north of the north-eastern tip of Korea near the border of the U.S.S.R.).

Between 30 and 50 atomic bombs would have more than done the job. Dropped under cover of darkness they would have destroyed the enemy's air force on the ground, wiped out his maintenance and his airmen. His only means of rebuilding would have been over the single-track Trans-Siberian Railroad. It is an excellently run railroad but it could not have handled the material needed to rebuild the enemy's air force in a sufficient space of time.

With the destruction of the enemy's air power I would then have called upon 500,000 of Chiang Kai-shek's troops, sweetened by two United States Marine divisions. These would have been formed into two amphibious forces. One, totaling four-fifths of my strength and led by one of the Marine divisions, would have landed at Antung and proceeded eastward along the road that parallels the Yalu.

[1] From the *New York Times* (April 9, 1964): p. 16. Copyright © 1964, 1951 by the New York Times Company. Reprinted by permission.

The other force, led by the other Marine division, would have landed simultaneously at Unggi or Najin, hit the same river road, and charged very quickly westward. Forces could have joined in two days, forming a wall of manpower and fire-power across the northern border of Korea. I had nearly all the shipping I needed, in Japan, and could have procured the rest from Pearl Harbor. That was no problem.

Now, the Eighth Army, spread along the 38th Parallel, would have put pressure on the enemy from the south. The joined amphibious forces would press down from the north.

Nothing in the way of supplies or reinforcements could have moved across the Yalu. North Korea, holding not less than one million to one million and a half of the enemy, could not have sustained him. It had been picked clean.

The enemy commander would have been starved out within 10 days after the landings. I suggest now he would have sued for peace immediately after learning his air had been taken out and we had spread across his supply routes.

You may ask what would have prevented the enemy's reinforcements massing and crossing the Yalu in great strength.

It was my plan as our amphibious forces moved south to spread behind us—from the Sea of Japan to the Yellow Sea—a belt of radioactive cobalt. It could have been spread from wagons, carts, trucks and planes. It is not an expensive material. It has an active life of between 60 and 120 years.

For at least 60 years there could have been no land invasion of Korea from the north. The enemy could not have marched across that radiated belt.

Russia? It makes me laugh when I recall the fears of the Truman-Acheson-Marshall-Bradley-general staff group that Russia would commit its armies to a war in China's behalf at the end of an endless one-track railroad to a peninsular battleground that led only to the sea.

Russia could not have engaged us. She would not have fought for China. She is already unhappy and uncertain over the colossus she has encouraged. The truce we entered into—that stupendous blunder of refusing to win when we could have won—has given China the breathing time she needed.

Primitive airfields in Manchuria have been transformed into modern installations with 10,000-foot runways.

China had only one concentrated arms-producing area before Mr. Truman relieved me. Now she has built or is in the process of building four more. In 50 years, if she can develop her plane-building facilities, China will be one of the world's top military powers.

It was in our power to destroy the Red Chinese army and Chinese military power. And probably for all time. My plan was a cinch. I was refused the right to carry it out by a group of isolationists and the politically minded joint chiefs.

You may be surprised to hear Truman, Acheson, Marshall and the others called isolationists. They were the true isolationists. They made only one revision in what we came to know as isolationism in this country. They expanded their walls to include Western Europe. They never comprehended the world as a whole. They never understood the enormous forces of Asia.

Under Eisenhower—a naive and honest man who does not want to offend anyone—we have maintained that isolationism. In time, we will scuttle our holdings and interests in the Pacific.

16

Render Unto God That Which Is His (1955)[1]

MacArthur was a man of great religious interests, and his public statements often sounded a missionary note. On January 26, 1955, he told the 60th annual convention of the Episcopal Diocese of Los Angeles of his attempts to foster the religious rehabilitation of Japan.

Much of my life has been dedicated to the profession of arms. Much of my experience has been in the practice of the arts of destruction. For such a one it is a rare privilege, indeed, when an occasion arises permitting construction rather than destruction—to build not to destroy. Such was the unusual and unique opportunity presenting itself in the field of religion when our victorious troops entered Japan. These were veteran soldiers; soldiers who had come from behind; soldiers constantly outnumbered and consequently constantly operating in the shadow of death. Now they had come through against all odds and were duly thankful to a merciful God. They were spiritual to the highest degree—the most religious army of modern times—men who prayed before they fought; men who built their churches even before they built their hospitals. Japan, itself, was in a state of utter collapse. It was completely exhausted. Its long war effort had reduced its industrial potential to almost nothing. Its military defeat had destroyed not only its sense of self-reliance but its sense of self-respect. Its religious disintegration was even worse. It was universal and absolute. In this vacuum, material, social and spiritual, the occupation began. Three concepts of divinity existed in Japan prior to the war: Shintoism, bred of the native culture of the Japanese race; Buddhism, introduced from the Asiatic mainland; and Christianity, an Occidental importation, a poor third. The latter's influence became negligible during the war. The first two were practically taken over by the government as a means of regimentation of the masses. The priesthood represented one of the most cultured, influential and intellectual segments of society, but was dominated by the state. The temples were supported by national funds, and the priests themselves,

[1] Reprinted by permission of the Bureau of Archives, MacArthur Memorial.

for all practical purposes, were but agents of those in political power. Under government tutelage the people were thoroughly indoctrinated with a belief in the invincible character of their armed forces. The propaganda was complete and no Japanese up to the very end dreamed of anything but victory. The shock of sudden defeat was thus enormously increased and left the populace doubtful and resentful, not only of their military and political leaders but of their religions as well.

I am a Christian—an Episcopalian—but I believe in all religions. They may differ in form and ritual, but all are good—all recognize a Divine Creator—a spiritual power transcending all that is mortal. I, therefore, felt that it became my duty as a soldier of God to attempt to restore and revive religion in Japan—to fill this moral vacuum— just as it was my duty as a soldier of the republic to revitalize the general welfare of the country; that to fulfill my obligation it must be of the spirit as well as of the flesh. But the problem was how? Should I with full military power arbitrarily decree the adoption of the Christian faith as a national religion? Like all men of human frailty in their hour of defeat and despairing agony, I knew they must turn to some higher spiritual power for comfort and support. Would not this be the moment to order them to abandon their own and to turn to our God? Their helplessness, their dire necessity born of complete disaster and dependence would have perhaps forced an outward compliance, but it would have been but a fictitious and superficial sham and would have surely defeated the very purpose in mind. The solution I adopted I believe you would have approved. It was to befriend all religions, to permit complete freedom of worship as individuals might choose, to free all creeds—Shinto, Buddhist and Christian— from any government control, to stop all proselytizing of the church by national subsidy, to restore to the temples their fundamental obligation of religious tutelage, to make the priest no longer an agent of political coercion or of espionage activity. In short, to render unto God that which is his and not unto Caesar that which he would.

It worked like a charm. The priesthood responded to their release from governmental dominance with a spiritual fervor which swept all before it. No slave passing to freedom ever exceeded their buoyant reaction. The religious vacuum disappeared. And, because I was Christian and had acted so, it aroused among the Shintoists and Buddhists a great curiosity of the religion that had dictated my decision. Their creeds, good in part as they were, were based to some extent on a *quid pro quo* concept—that one should do good in this life because he would profit from it in the life to come; that he would be repaid; that he would get back more than he put in—reward in another world was a main incentive. The concept of faith—the concept of Christ—that a man should do what was right even if it meant personal sacrifice; that the urge of conscience was greater than any material reward—was something new and novel. It seemed to me the great opportunity was to guide Shintoism and Buddhism toward the basic concept of Christian faith rather than the impossible task of replacement by a conqueror's own creed; that if the immutable lessons of the Scriptures—of the Sermon on the Mount—could be integrated and welded into their own religious cultures—if basic morality could be common to all—it would mean little whether a Japanese were a Shintoist, a Buddhist or a Christian.

I called upon America for Bibles. An offer of a hundred thousand was raised by me to ten million with an ultimate figure of three times that number. And that is the story up to now.

I am not trained in ecclesiastical methods nor am I skilled in theological lore, but I want you to know with such frail personal equipment as was mine I did my best; and that no phase of the occupation —with its many attempted military, political, social and economic reforms—has left me with a greater sense of personal satisfaction than my spiritual stewardship. Although I am of Caesar, I did try to render unto God that which was his. And I even dare to hope that through this resurgence of religion, Japan will in the struggle that lies ahead be indissolubly confirmed against any whose doctrines embrace the deadly poison of atheism. It might prove more potent than bullets or bayonets or bombs—or even bread.

17

Our Confiscatory Tax System Via Karl Marx (1958)[1]

In the last years of his life, MacArthur grew increasingly conservative on economic issues. Here he denounces federal spending and the income tax.

Whether we want it or not, we pay now for almost unlimited government—but a government which delimits our lives by dictating how we are fed, and clothed, and housed; how to provide for our old age; how the national income, which is the product of our labor, shall be divided among us; how we shall buy and sell, how long and how hard and under what circumstances we shall work. There is only scorn for the one who dares to say the Government should not be infinite.

Bureaucrats rule us. They no longer believe that free men can manage their own affairs. Their central thesis is to take your money away from you on the presumption that a handful of men, centered in government, largely bureaucratic—not elected—can spend the proceeds of your toil and labor to greater advantage than you who create the money. Nowhere in the history of the human race is there justification for this reckless faith in political power.

Excessive taxation produces results resembling evils of slavery and serfdom in the days of old. To illustrate: The Government takes in taxes over a third of the income of the average citizen each year. . . . It is indeed the modern although humanized counterpart, in the twentieth century, of the abandoned slavery and serfdom of the preceding centuries.

The Russian dictator, Lenin, that implacable foe of the free enterprise system, predicted as early as 1920 that the United States would eventually spend itself into bankruptcy. Inflation is not a question of partisan politics. It can be controlled only if political parties really wish to stop it—only if both parties are determined to limit spending so as to be within our means.

If financial output has to be increased in one segment, it must be correspondingly decreased in another. If defense spending has to go

[1] From Douglas MacArthur, "Our Confiscatory Tax System Via Karl Marx," *The American Mercury*, 87 (January, 1958): 63–64. Reprinted by permission of *The American Mercury*.

up, other spending, whether for housing, schools or social benefits, must be curtailed accordingly.

The problem, a balanced budget, instead of being a mystic and untouchable phenomenon, is actually the commonest and most universal one in the world. It faces the head of every household every year of life. . . .

Our swollen budgets constantly have been misrepresented to the public. . . . Taxation, with its offspring, inflation, said Lenin in support of the basic thesis of Karl Marx, is the vital weapon to displace the system of free enterprise. Lenin meant the system on which our nation was founded; the system which has made us the most prosperous people of all history; the system which enabled us to produce over half of the world's goods with less than one-seventh of the world's area and population; the system which gave our people more liberty and opportunities than any other nation ever gave its people in the long history of the world.

The fundamental and ultimate issue at stake therefore is not merely our money—it is liberty itself: the excessive taxation of an overgrown government versus personal freedom. The least common denominator of mediocrity against the proven progress of pioneering individualism. The free enterprise system or the cult of blind conformity. The robot or the free man.

18
Duty, Honor, Country (1962)[1]

On May 12, 1962, MacArthur visited West Point to receive the Sylvanus Thayer Award and to participate in the ceremonies of the day. After being presented with the award, MacArthur made this statement to the Corps of Cadets. Delivered extemporaneously, it is an eloquent summary of the code of honor of the professional soldier.

No human being could fail to be deeply moved by such a tribute as this. Coming from a profession I have served so long and a people I have loved so well, it fills me with an emotion I cannot express. But this award is not intended primarily to honor a personality, but to symbolize a great moral code—a code of conduct and chivalry of those who guard this beloved land of culture and ancient descent. For all hours and for all time, it is an expression of the ethics of the American soldier. That I should be integrated in this way with so noble an ideal arouses a sense of pride, and yet of humility, which will be with me always.

Duty, honor, country: Those three hallowed words reverently dictate what you ought to be, what you can be, what you will be. They are your rallying point to build courage when courage seems to fail, to regain faith when there seems to be little cause for faith, to create hope when hope becomes forlorn.

Unhappily, I possess neither that eloquence of diction, that poetry of imagination, nor that brilliance of metaphor to tell you all that they mean.

The unbelievers will say they are but words, but a slogan, but a flamboyant phrase. Every pedant, every demagogue, every cynic, every hypocrite, every troublemaker, and, I am sorry to say, some others of an entirely different character, will try to downgrade them even to the extent of mockery and ridicule.

But these are some of the things they do. They build your basic character. They mold you for your future roles as the custodians of the nation's defense. They make you strong enough to know when you are weak, and brave enough to face yourself when you are afraid.

[1] From *Vital Speeches of the Day*, 28 (June 15, 1962): 519–21. Reprinted by permission of the publisher.

They teach you to be proud and unbending in honest failure, but humble and gentle in success; not to substitute words for actions, not to seek the path of comfort, but to face the stress and spur of difficulty and challenge; to learn to stand up in the storm, but to have compassion on those who fall; to master yourself before you seek to master others; to have a heart that is clean, a goal that is high; to learn to laugh, yet never forget how to weep; to reach into the future, yet never neglect the past; to be serious, yet never to take yourself too seriously; to be modest so that you will remember the simplicity of true greatness, the open mind of true wisdom, the meekness of true strength.

They give you a temperate will, a quality of the imagination, a vigor of the emotions, a freshness of the deep springs of life, a temperamental predominance of courage over timidity, of an appetite for adventure over love of ease.

They create in your heart the sense of wonder, the unfailing hope of what next, and the joy and inspiration of life. They teach you in this way to be an officer and a gentleman. . . .

The code which those words perpetuate embraces the highest moral law and will stand the test of any ethics or philosophies ever promulgated for the uplift of mankind. Its requirements are for the things that are right and its restraints are from the things that are wrong. The soldier, above all other men, is required to practice the greatest act of religious training—sacrifice. In battle, and in the face of danger and death, he discloses those divine attributes which his Maker gave when He created man in His own image. No physical courage and no greater strength can take the place of the divine help which alone can sustain him. However hard the incidents of war may be, the soldier who is called upon to offer and to give his life for his country is the noblest development of mankind.

You now face a new world, a world of change. The thrust into outer space of the satellite spheres and missiles marks a beginning of another epoch in the long story of mankind. In the 5 or more billions of years the scientists tell us it has taken to form the earth, in the 3 or more billion years of development of the human race, there has never been a more abrupt or staggering evolution.

We deal now, not with things of this world alone, but with the illimitable distances and as yet unfathomed mysteries of the universe. We are reaching out for a new and boundless frontier. We speak in strange terms of harnessing the cosmic energy; of making winds and tides work for us; of creating unheard-of synthetic materials to supplement or even replace our old standard basics, to purify sea water for our drink; of mining ocean floors for new fields of wealth and food; of disease preventives to expand life into the hundreds of years; of controlling the weather for a more equitable distribution of heat and cold, of rain and shine; of spaceships to the moon; of the primary target in war no longer limited to the armed forces of an enemy, but instead to include his civil populations; of ultimate conflict between a united human race and the sinister forces of some other planetary galaxy; of such dreams and fantasies as to make life the most exciting of all times.

And through all this welter of change and development your mission remains fixed, determined, inviolable. It is to win our wars. Everything else in your professional career is but corollary to this vital dedication. All other public purposes, all other public projects, all other public needs, great or small, will find others for their accomplishment; but you are the ones who are trained to fight.

Yours is the profession of arms, the will to win, the sure knowledge that in war there is no substitute for victory, that if you lose, the nation will be destroyed, that the very obsession of your public service must be duty, honor, country.

Others will debate the controversial issues, national and international, which divide men's minds. But serene, calm, aloof, you stand as the nation's war guardian, as its lifeguard from the raging tides of international conflict, as its gladiator in the arena of battle. For a century and a half you have defended, guarded, and protected its hallowed traditions of liberty and freedom, of right and justice.

Let civilian voices argue the merits or demerits of our processes of government: Whether our strength is being sapped by deficit financing indulged in too long, by Federal paternalism grown too mighty, by power groups grown too arrogant, by politics grown too corrupt, by crime grown too rampant, by morals grown too low, by taxes grown too high, by extremists grown too violent; whether our personal liberties are as thorough and complete as they should be.

These great national problems are not for your professional participation or military solution. Your guidepost stands out like a tenfold beacon in the night: Duty, honor, country.

You are the leaven which binds together the entire fabric of our national system of defense. From your ranks come the great captains who hold the nation's destiny in their hands the moment the war tocsin sounds.

The long grey line has never failed us. Were you to do so, a million

ghosts in olive drab, in brown khaki, in blue and grey, would rise
from their white crosses, thundering those magic words: Duty, honor,
country.

This does not mean that you are warmongers. On the contrary, the
soldier above all other people prays for peace, for he must suffer and
bear the deepest wounds and scars of war. But always in our ears ring
the ominous words of Plato, that wisest of all philosophers: "Only
the dead have seen the end of war."

The shadows are lengthening for me. The twilight is here. My days
of old have vanished—tone and tint. They have gone glimmering
through the dreams of things that were. Their memory is one of
wondrous beauty, watered by tears and coaxed and caressed by the
smiles of yesterday. I listen vainly, but with thirsty ear, for the witching melody of faint bugles blowing reveille, of far drums beating the
long roll.

In my dreams I hear again the crash of guns, the rattle of musketry,
the strange, mournful mutter of the battlefield. But in the evening
of my memory always I come back to West Point. Always there echoes
and re-echoes: Duty, honor, country.

Today marks my final rollcall with you. But I want you to know
that, when I cross the river, my last conscious thoughts will be of the
corps, and the corps, and the corps.

I bid you farewell.

DOUGLAS MACARTHUR
VIEWED BY HIS CONTEMPORARIES

19
From Peace to War,
1933-1941

*As the United States Army chief of staff in the early
1930s, MacArthur asked Major Dwight D. Eisenhower to serve
as his personal aide. Eisenhower recalled that, beginning in January, 1933, he worked as "an amanuensis to draft statements, reports, and letters" for MacArthur's signature. When MacArthur
moved on to the Philippines, Eisenhower accompanied him, remaining on his staff until December, 1939. In Manila, MacArthur
became acquainted with the United States High Commissioner
to the Philippines, Francis B. Sayre, who encountered many of
the difficulties of William Howard Taft with another MacArthur
years before. In November, 1941, Major General Lewis H. Brereton travelled to the Philippines, at MacArthur's request, to serve
as his air commander. Brereton would witness the devastating
Japanese attack on Clark Field—the first of a series of blows
that would drive MacArthur in retreat from his Manila outpost
to Australia.*

DWIGHT D. EISENHOWER: WORKING FOR MACARTHUR
IN WASHINGTON AND MANILA[1]

Douglas MacArthur was a forceful—some thought an overpowering—individual, blessed with a fast and facile mind, interested in both
the military and political side of our government. From the beginning,
I found that he was well acquainted with most of the people in
government in almost every department. Working with him brought

[1] From Dwight D. Eisenhower, *At Ease: Stories I Tell to Friends* (Garden City,
N.Y.: Doubleday & Company, Inc., 1967), pp. 312–15, 223–26. Copyright © 1967 by
Dwight D. Eisenhower. Reprinted by permission of Doubleday & Company, Inc.,
and Robert Hale & Company.

an additional dimension to my experience. My duties were beginning to verge on the political, even to the edge of partisan politics.

Most of the senior officers I had known always drew a clean-cut line between the military and the political. Off duty, among themselves and close civilian friends, they might explosively denounce everything they thought was wrong in Washington and the world, and propose their own cure for its evils. On duty, nothing could induce them to cross the line they, and old Army tradition, had established. But if General MacArthur ever recognized the existence of that line, he usually chose to ignore it. At times, this could complicate life for himself and his staff.

My office was next to his; only a slatted door separated us. He called me to his office by raising his voice. When I had visitors in my office, I always made sure that the door was closed because I didn't want to disturb the General. At the time he was fifty-three. He was decisive, personable, and he had one habit that never ceased to startle me. In reminiscing or in telling stories of the current scene, he talked of himself in the third person. "So MacArthur went over to the Senator, and said, 'Senator . . .'" Although I had heard of this idiosyncrasy, the sensation was unusual. In time I got used to it and saw it not as objectionable, just odd.

On any subject he chose to discuss, his knowledge, always amazingly comprehensive, and largely accurate, poured out in a torrent of words. "Discuss" is hardly the correct word; discussion suggests dialogue and the General's conversations were usually monologues.

One of the General's old friends, who had a fifteen-minute interview with him, sat and listened to him and was able to insert only an occasional yes or no. The Colonel left the office and realized that under the MacArthur treatment he had forgotten to bring up the subject of his visit.

Later that day, encountering another officer whose appointment with MacArthur had immediately followed his, the officer said: "You certainly made a tremendous impression on General MacArthur."

The Colonel, bewildered as he recalled the one-sided nature of the talk, asked, "What in the world do you mean?"

The other officer replied: "Why, the General said when I went in that he had just had a tremendously interesting chat with you. He said that he always looks forward to your visits because you are a fascinating conversationalist from whom he learns a great deal!"

Unquestionably, the General's fluency and wealth of information came from his phenomenal memory, without parallel in my knowledge. Reading through a draft of a speech or a paper once, he could immediately repeat whole chunks of it verbatim.

In several respects, he was a rewarding man to work for. When he gave an assignment, he never asked any questions; he never cared what kind of hours were kept; his only requirement was that the work be done. The difficulty was that I soon found myself engaged in a variety of reports, statements, estimates, and the like that kept me so busy I was in the office until 7:30 or 7:45 every night. Because General MacArthur kept unusual hours, including luncheons or other absences from two to four hours and then stayed on in his office until 8:00, my hours became picturesque. But if the occasion came up for me to take a week's leave, all I had to do was tell him I was going away for a few days and he would make no objection.

Of course, the work did pile up while I was gone. . . .

Whether or not those of us in the small group that departed Washington for Manila thought that we were on a singular and striking mission—a great power was deliberately and voluntarily proposing to arm and train a dependent people—I don't recall. Even though our Chief, Douglas MacArthur, spoke and wrote in purple splendor, his subordinates were restrained in the language we used about the future. We played it down as just another job.

We knew we would be scraping for pennies and pesos. In the judgment of outsiders, of course, the presence of General MacArthur outweighed limitless amounts of money and men. Unhappily, at the very outset, he suffered two shocks.

The first struck while we were still en route to the West Coast. One moment Douglas MacArthur was Chief of Staff of the United States Army, whose arrival in Manila would be dramatic testimony that our country considered Philippine independence and defense so important that the head of our Army had been sent there to help; and the next moment, after he tore open a telegram from Washington and read it in silence, he learned that he was now only a former Chief of Staff, and was reduced from four-star to two-star rank.

Firmly fixed in the General's mind was the conviction that President Roosevelt had agreed to retain him in the top position until a month after his arrival in Manila. The prestige of those four stars in the eyes of the Filipinos would have been a certain help, he thought. He would be retiring as Chief of Staff to aid the new cause. Suddenly, out of the clear at an isolated railroad station hundreds of miles from Washington, to learn that a new COS had been appointed caused him to express himself freely. It was an explosive denunciation of politics, bad manners, bad judgment, broken promises, arrogance, unconstitutionality, insensitivity, and the way the world had gone to hell. Then he sent an eloquent telegram of congratulations to his successor.

In the long run, except for personal resentments, no harm may have been done to our mission. The second blow, falling months later, had a more deeply personal effect. It deprived the General of a lifelong source of inspiration and strength, his mother.

The widow of General Arthur MacArthur was among the most remarkable of Army wives and mothers. All her life she had been with the Army on the frontier and in the Pacific, as well as in Washington. She was imbued with assurance that her son was destined for greatness; she lived for him and his success. Despite his own immense talents, the General relied heavily on her when the going was tough; he shared with her as a partner the joys of achievement. . . .

From the outset, the work was difficult. We tried to figure new and better ways to provide a reasonable defense establishment once the Islands were on their own. This meant that the Islands would have to be dependent to some extent upon the United States government, upon its generosity and readiness to accept the security of the Philippines as a matter of vital interest to the United States. We worked full tilt to polish up drafts of the necessary law, getting advice from Philippine legislators. As soon as the law was passed, we started to build little training stations—nothing more than barracks and cleared spaces in various sections of the Islands. To minimize transportation costs we built more than ninety of these stations, with about two hundred conscripts in each place.

We soon saw that it was necessary to have a small "air force" even if for nothing else than to get to the training stations. The roadnet of the Philippines archipelago, comprising something over seven thousand islands, was still primitive except in Luzon. Light planes that could land and take off from short strips would make every training site accessible.

So, aiming at two birds with one stone, we bought a few primary trainers of the type used at Randolph Field and borrowed two instructors from the Army Air Corps.

Though we worked doggedly through 1936 and 1937, ours was a hopeless venture, in a sense. The Philippine government simply could not afford to build real security from attack. We had to content ourselves with an attempt to produce a military adequate to deal with domestic revolt and to provide at least a passive type of defense around the perimeter of the Islands to slow up the advance of any aggressor until some friendly nation, presumably the United States, came to their aid.

We were encountering then an example of the costs of independence that others have met more recently when so many dependent colonies find themselves on their own and a little bit intoxicated by freedom. Too many Filipinos, even those high in government, were concerned with the privileges of independence and too little with its responsibilities and costs. Often President Quezon and I talked this over. He had prepared a private office for me in his Malacañan Palace because of the amount of work I had to do between his office and ours as liaison agent. He understood but insisted that national pride would demand that they have at least some kind of military force.

Then there was an incident that chilled the warm relationship that Jimmy Ord and I had with General MacArthur. The General had an idea that the morale of the whole population would be enhanced if the people could see something of their emerging army in the capital city, Manila. He suggested a large demonstration of strength, bringing units from all over the Islands to a field near the city, and camping them there for three or four days. The city's population could visit them and it would all end with a big parade.

Jimmy and I estimated the cost. We told the General that it was impossible to do the thing within our budget. Carrying out this demonstration would take money that was desperately needed for more important purposes. But following the General's orders, we began to do the necessary staff work.

Among other details, we had to arrange with island shipping firms to bring in the troops. It wasn't long until news of this reached the Philippine government. President Quezon called me in from the little office in Malacañan, said he had heard about the planned troop movement, and asked me what it was all about.

I was astonished. We had assumed that the project had first been agreed on between the President and General MacArthur. When I discovered that this was not the case, I told Quezon that I thought we should discuss it no further until I could see General MacArthur. But Quezon was disturbed and said he was going to telephone the General. I said I would withdraw to my office and when he wanted me again, he could reach me there.

He didn't call and I returned to my other office in the Walled City within the hour. General MacArthur was exceedingly unhappy with his entire staff. By the time I saw him, he was visibly upset. He said he had never meant for us to proceed with preparations for the parade. He had only wanted us to investigate it quietly. Now the matter had come to the ears of the President who was horrified to think that we were ready for a costly national parade in the capital. Because General MacArthur denied he had given us an order—which was certainly news to us—there was nothing to do except stop the proceedings. This misunderstanding caused considerable resentment—and never again were we on the same warm and cordial terms.

FRANCIS B. SAYRE: WITH MACARTHUR IN THE PHILIPPINES [2]

Tall, spare, with a thin face, receding dark hair, piercing eyes, and low, resonant voice, he gave the impression of drama in his bearing, his action, and his words. Sharp and observant though his glance, he seemed always indrawn and playing his part as a great actor. Although never seeming to lose himself in an emotional outburst, he was a skillful orator, conscious always of the effect upon his listeners. With his keen trenchant mind and his far-reaching knowledge of history and of military strategy as part of history, he could hold listeners spellbound.

Having lived in Manila several years before our arrival, he had a tight circle of loyal aides and admirers. As a man of strong, positive character, he naturally had enemies, too. To the average American in Manila who saw him always from the distance—for he held himself aloof from the crowd—he gave the effect of being inscrutable and enigmatic. His personality lacked the open, demoncratic, American approach.

In contrast the spontaneous warmth and genuine friendliness of his wife were of immense help to him. Americans and Filipinos alike were won by her charm and her soft, Southern voice. In their social life she knew well how to protect and uphold "the General," as she always called him even to intimate friends. They had married rather late in the General's life; and now with their three-year-old son, Arthur, their happiness seemed complete in their ivory tower atop the Manila Hotel.

Until his appointment as head of USAFFE my contacts with Gen-

[2] From Francis B. Sayre, *Glad Adventure* (New York: The Macmillan Company, 1957), pp. 207–209. Copyright © 1957 by Francis B. Sayre. Reprinted by permission of The Macmillan Company.

eral MacArthur were social rather than official. One of his early communications was a very personal note delivered by an aide. At a large luncheon for ladies which my wife had given at the residence to the Red Cross volunteers, Mrs. MacArthur had not been seated with what the General considered to be a proper observance of her rank. Adverting to "recent circumstances," he set forth his understanding as to the proper rank which should be accorded to him and his wife. I sent back a note telling of my entire ignorance of the incident, adding that there was no intent to alter her rank and assuring him that his wife would always be accorded in my home all the honor due her. This the General immediately acknowledged with an appreciative and warmly expressed, hand-written reply. . . .

President Quezon, as the months passed, had apparently lost confidence in the judgment of his military adviser, and more than once in a public address squarely contradicted previous positive declarations made by General MacArthur. Quezon, as I knew from personal experience, could be extremely temperamental. But his attitude toward the General, so far as one could see, was due more to fundamental loss of confidence than to superficial disagreements. To an exceedingly important conference held in Baguio between President Quezon, representing the Philippines, and myself representing the United States, to shape up general defense plans, I naturally invited General Grunert, in command of American forces in the Philippines, to be present and take a leading part in our discussions. I had expected that President Quezon would call in General MacArthur as his adviser; but to my surprise he did not do so and in our discussion the General was not referred to. According to the current talk of Manila, General MacArthur's star was rapidly descending and he was expected to drop out of the Philippine picture. His assistant and chief of staff, Colonel Dwight Eisenhower, whom we all liked and respected, had already asked for his transfer to Washington, and departed soon after our arrival.

However, all this was changed on July 26, 1941, when President Roosevelt ordered the incorporation of the Philippine armed forces in the United States Army and appointed General MacArthur Commander of the United States Armed Forces in the Far East. His appointment fell like a bombshell on Manila. From that time on President Quezon gave to General MacArthur loyal cooperation and support. General MacArthur at once set about a progressive incorporation of the reserve forces of the Philippine Army into the service of the United States.

LEWIS H. BRERETON: THE ROAD TO WAR [3]

MANILA, 10 November 1941. In talks with General MacArthur before leaving for Australia, I got the impression that his belief in 1 April as the earliest probable date when hostilities might commence had been severely shaken since my earlier conferences with him. I think that he was particularly impressed by the fact that [special Japanese envoy Saburo] Kurusu, who had previously been discredited by his own government, had been called back from retirement to go to Washington. General MacArthur's feeling was that Kurusu was being used as a stooge and that unless the talks in Washington were favorable to Japan he would again be discredited. General MacArthur had more insight into the Japanese political situation than anyone else I knew.

I noticed again one of General MacArthur's traits: he cannot talk sitting down. It seems to me that the more clearly he enunciates his ideas, the more vigorous his walking becomes. He is one of the most beautiful talkers I have ever heard and, while his manner might be considered a bit on the theatrical side, it is just a part of his personality and an expression of his character. There is never any doubt as to what he means and what he wants.

Another impressive characteristic is General MacArthur's immaculate appearance. He is one of the best-dressed soldiers in the world. Even in the hot tropical climate of Manila, where we wore cotton shirts and trousers which for most people became wet and wilted in an hour, I have never seen him looking otherwise than as if he had just put on a fresh uniform. . . .

MANILA, 24 December 1941. On the afternoon of Christmas Eve I was called by General MacArthur for a conference. He expressed his extreme gratification over the part the Far East Air Force had taken in the battle of Luzon and told me that I was being ordered to proceed south with my Headquarters. I asked to remain on his staff in any capacity in which he could use me.

"No, Lewis," he said. "You go on south. You can do me more good with the bombers you have left and those you should be receiving soon than you can here. Since communications over that distance are

[3] From Lewis H. Brereton, *The Brereton Diaries* (New York: William Morrow & Company, Inc., 1946), pp. 24–25, 61–62. Reprinted by permission of William Morrow & Company, Inc., and Paul R. Reynolds, Inc.

practically impossible now, I must depend to the greatest extent upon your own initiative to support our forces here."

I rose and prepared to leave, and General MacArthur said, "I hope that you will tell the people outside what we have done and protect my reputation as a fighter."

As I shook hands with him I said, "General, your reputation will never need any protection."

20
MacArthur in World War II

MacArthur owed much of his popularity to his dramatic role in the Second World War. At a time when warfare had become increasingly drab and mechanized, the colorful pronouncements from MacArthur's command provided stirring news stories for consumption on the home front. Furthermore, much of the chronicling of MacArthur's wartime activity was done by zealous members of his staff, such as Major Generals Charles A. Willoughby and George C. Kenney. As a result, public opinion surveys at the end of the war revealed him to be second only to Eisenhower as the most admired figure in the United States armed forces. He retained his traditional conservative following, including many former isolationists finding their new cause in an "Asia-First" policy, and added the plaudits of many liberals, who appreciated his determination to win a war which they wholeheartedly endorsed. Criticism did emerge, however, in a few almost-forgotten ballads drafted by members of the armed forces, resentful of the general's extraordinary public relations image. Indeed, polls taken in 1946 revealed that a large majority of World War II veterans opposed MacArthur as a Presidential candidate, with the largest majority from the general's own Pacific command.

CHARLES A. WILLOUGHBY: MACARTHUR'S WARTIME STRATEGY [1]

When the Japanese attacked the Philippines on December 8, 1941, Gen. Douglas MacArthur, who had been named Commander of the United States Armed Forces in the Far East on July 27, was still in the midst of a zealous eleventh-hour struggle to build up enough "muscle" to repel the enemy. He had spent six years in the islands as military adviser to Manuel Quezon—which was four years short of the time he deemed necessary to build the Filipino Army into a fighting force competent to throw the troops of a major invading power into the sea. Starved for funds that were anywhere near commensurate with preparations for modern warfare, MacArthur lacked the guns, planes, and PT boats that might have made the inland waters of the

[1] From Charles A. Willoughby and John Chamberlain, *MacArthur, 1941–1951* (New York: McGraw-Hill Book Company, 1954), pp. 16–17, 78–79, 280–81. Reprinted by permission of the author.

1,400 islands impregnable and the outer beaches a terrible hazard to the presumptive invader. Nor had the United States sent him much after making him chief of USAFFE in July. A few P-40s and Flying Fortresses, a small fleet of PTs, a few trained officers, two transport loads of troop reinforcements—and that was about all.

Nevertheless, the combined Filipino and American forces held out in Bataan and Corregidor for virtually six months, denying Manila Bay to an enemy that was frantic to use the local docks as staging intermediaries in its thrusts to the South Seas. That six-month period of successful delaying action was precisely the task set for the Filipino-American forces in the Orange Plan for the defense of the Philippines. In the Orange Plan, the Navy was counted on to lift the siege of the islands within a half a year. . . .

In the latter days of the Pacific war, the Americans held a technological advantage over the Japanese that did much to offset the discrepancy in sheer manpower. But in the Philippines from December 1941 to April 1942 MacArthur was forced back on the intangibles of will, heart, and intellect. Besides the fighting stamina of his men, the General had two things on his side that were worth many divisions. The first was his knowledge of the Japanese mind—a knowledge that dated back to the days of the Russo-Japanese War when he was an observer in Manchuria with his father, Gen. Arthur MacArthur. The second was an encyclopedic knowledge of previous campaigns in the Philippines. . . . Knowledge of the first helped MacArthur to parlay the second into the long six-month struggle to hold Bataan and Corregidor, which saved the day until Allied defenses could be reorganized in Australia. . . .

MacArthur has never seen fit to grade the big Pacific war decisions in the order of their importance. But, quite aside from Roosevelt's decision to move him from Corregidor to Australia, there are three moves made by the General, in spite of opposition, in the early days of the war that were basic, momentous, and ultimately decisive. The first, as we have seen, was the sideslip from Manila into Bataan, which delayed the Japanese southward thrusts by as much as six months. The second big decision, made at a time when practically every able-bodied Australian thought only to die with his boots on at the Brisbane Line, was, according to MacArthur, to "stop the enemy advances along the Owen Stanley Ridge in New Guinea." This saved Australia from invasion, changed the whole attitude from one of defense to offense, and changed the national morale from despair and defeatism to confidence and victory. And the third crucial decision was to push an "arrow-straight" advance from New Guinea to the Philippines, thus accomplishing a practical unity of our divided command in the Pacific, preventing a dispersion of our forces and objectives, which might well have led to disasters through attacks by a concentrated enemy on our scattered and far-flung units, and greatly reducing our losses by avoiding unnecessary and corollary battles.

Since the second and third big decisions were really phases of a single grand strategy, which he had in his mind as early as March 1942, MacArthur usually brackets them when talking about the Pacific war. The curious thing about it is that the Navy high command in Washington never recognized the relationship between the decision to hold the Owen Stanley Line and the decision to retake the Philippines. The Navy Department saw the Pacific as its own peculiar war: the old Orange Plan had envisaged a westward passage of ships and a great naval victory, to be followed by a rescue or a bypassing of the Philippines and an eventual investment of Japan; and even after the eruption of the Japanese into the Solomon Islands the Navy Department held stubbornly to an Orange Plan revival. Stung by Pearl Harbor, the Navy wanted the lion's share of the fight. In their view, MacArthur's job was to hold in New Guinea, to help out in the Solomons, and then to press westward along the Malay Barrier toward the Indies and Singapore. A side expedition to Mindanao might have been permitted as an offshoot of such a movement, but certainly nothing more.

MacArthur was adamant against this sort of thinking from the very beginning, and fortunately his views prevailed. . . .

In all of the Philippine operations General MacArthur was habitually at the front. His continual exposure to enemy view was an incessant source of anxiety and worry to his staff. On one occasion, when his G-2 remonstrated with him at his personal reconnoitering in front of our lines, his reply was a laconic, "Thanks, Charlie, but I can't fight 'em if I can't see 'em!"

In his twenty campaigns with their innumerable battles, covering six wars as a participant or an observer, MacArthur has received more medals for courage than any officer or man who had ever served in the American Army. . . .

To those who knew him well, what was even more remarkable than his extraordinary physical courage was his moral courage. He decided problems not on the basis of whether they would be popular or not, nor because of the possible effects on his own future, nor in response to influential pressures, but solely and simply on what he judged to be right or wrong. Emotionally sensitive to the rights of the lowly and absolutely devoted to the welfare of the nation, he was the very embodiment of the West Point tradition of "Duty, Honor, Country." Meticulous in carrying out the directives he received, he was fearless in his outspoken frankness of view in the discussion period preceding a final decision. And it was to be this patriotic candor and devoted fervor which ultimately cost him his command. But nothing has, or ever can, take from him a serenity of conscience and composure of deportment that are without peer.

WENDELL WILLKIE: BRING MACARTHUR HOME! (1942)[2]

To bring about effective cooperation one man should direct the military services. Ordinarily it might be hard, it might be almost impossible to find such a man.

But as the last two months have proved, we have the man—the one man in all our forces who has learned from first hand, contemporary experience the value and the proper use of Army, Navy, and air forces fighting together toward one end; the man who on Bataan Peninsula has accomplished what was regarded as the impossible by his brilliant tactical sense; the man who almost alone has given his fellow countrymen confidence and hope in the conduct of this war—General Douglas MacArthur.

MacArthur has long known the nature of this war. In 1933, when Chief of Staff, he foresaw the complete strategy of the Blitzkrieg as the method of modern warfare and so reported to the War Department. Steadily he carried on his fight against the opposition of Congress and of his fellow officers to convince them that the new war would demand a mechanized army; swift mobility of small units; and complete coordination of the air force for defense of coast lines, attack against ships and ground troops and for bombardment of supply lines. He argued that the new war would not be fought by an army or a navy or an air force, but by, and I want to quote from his report, "a nation at war, rather than a nation in arms" with the fighting forces "only the cutting edge"; he saw that a great proportion of the employable population would find its war duty in developing economic and industrial resources for an adequate munitions supply and the sustenance of the civilian population; he pointed out that "any major war

[2] From Wendell L. Willkie, "Let Us Do More Proposing Than Opposing," *Vital Speeches of the Day*, 8 (March 1, 1942): 299. Reprinted by permission of the publisher.

of the future will see every belligerent nation highly organized for the single purpose of victory."

Bring Douglas MacArthur home. Place him at the very top. Keep bureaucratic and political hands off him. Give him the responsibility and the power of coordinating all the armed forces of the nation to their most effective use. Put him in supreme command of our armed forces under the President.

Then the people of the United States will have reason to hope that skill, not bungling and confusion, directs their efforts.

THE *NATION* PRAISES MACARTHUR (1942) [3]

A wave of optimism has swept over the United Nations as a result of General MacArthur's assumption of supreme command in the Pacific. In part it may be attributed to the drama of his journey from the Philippines to Australia in the face of supposed Japanese mastery of the sea and air. Psychologically, the people of the United Nations needed just such a remarkable exploit to relieve the pessimism engendered by the seemingly never-ending series of Japanese successes. But fundamentally the optimism is based on a general recognition of MacArthur's abilities. Certainly no other military leader has yet appeared in the United Nations who possesses MacArthur's combination of experience in military leadership, knowledge of the Pacific area, and fighting qualities.

Considerable credit must be given to President Roosevelt for the decision to move MacArthur to his present post. It will be recalled that many of the anti-Administration newspapers had been urging that he be brought home to take charge of America's defenses. There had even been hints that the President was afraid to "save" MacArthur lest the General run against him in the 1944 elections. If anything had happened to MacArthur in his hazardous journey to Australia, we can be sure that these papers would have placed the responsibility directly upon Mr. Roosevelt. Yet the President took the risk because, as he himself pointed out, winning the war must come before all other considerations.

The first reaction in many circles to MacArthur's shift has been the assumption that the United Nations would now take the offensive against the Japanese. MacArthur himself seemed to confirm this assumption when he declared that he was sent "for the purpose . . . of organizing an American offensive against Japan." It would be un-

[3] From "A Pacific Offensive?" *Nation*, 154 (March 28, 1942): 356. Reprinted by permission of the publisher.

fortunate, however, if the public concluded from this statement that a large-scale offensive against the Japanese would be launched within the next few days or weeks. For the moment MacArthur is bound to have his hands much too full defending Australia to initiate any sweeping counterblows. During the coming weeks there may be periods when it will be nip and tuck whether Australia can be held. But if anyone can hold it, Douglas MacArthur is the man. His record in the Philippines shows that he can not only fight a skilful defensive battle against great odds but attack with vigor when the opportunity presents itself. We can be sure that in the midst of essentially defensive action, he will be planning the counterblows to be delivered as soon as his forces are adequate for the task.

A NAVY BALLAD [4]

For two long years, since blood and tears have been so very rife,
Confusion in our war news burdens more a soldier's life
But from this chaos, daily, like a hospice on the way,
Like a shining light to guide us, rises Doug's communiqué. . . .

'My battleships bombarded the Nips from Maine to Singapore
My subs have sunk a million tons; they'll sink a billion more.
My aircraft bombed Berlin last night.' In Italy they say,
'Our turn's tonight, because it's right in Doug's communiqué.' . . .

His area is quite cosmic and capricious as a breeze,
Ninety times as big as Texas, bigger than Los Angeles,
It springs from lost Atlantis up to where the angels play
And no sparrow falls unheeded—it's in Doug's communiqué.

GEORGE C. KENNEY: LANDING AT LEYTE (1944) [5]

When we landed at Leyte on October 20, 1944, MacArthur went ashore shortly after the assault waves had hit the beach and pushed a few hundred yards inland. A radio broadcasting station had been set up to announce the landing to the people of the Philippines and the rest of the world as well. MacArthur and President Osmena were scheduled to talk.

[4] From Richard H. Rovere and Arthur M. Schlesinger, Jr., *The General and the President* (New York: Farrar, Straus & Giroux, Inc., 1951), pp. 73–74. Copyright 1951 by Richard H. Rovere and Arthur M. Schlesinger, Jr. Reprinted by permission of the publisher.

[5] From George C. Kenney, *The MacArthur I Know* (New York: Duell, Sloan and Pearce, 1951), pp. 95–97. Reprinted by permission of Hawthorn Books, Inc.

The General's speech was immediately jumped on by his critics who called it "sacrilegious," "flamboyant," and "in poor taste." The word "corny" also came in for a lot of use. The stories also related, as a proof of MacArthur's supreme egotism, that he wanted to be the only one to make a speech on the occasion of his return to the Philippines, refusing to allow Admiral Thomas Kinkaid to talk, although as the naval commander he had had one already prepared and a recording made of it several days before the landing.

I was there. This is the complete story as I saw and heard it.

MacArthur's stirring appeal to the Filipino people to rally around him and expel the invader was the kind that makes the hair stand up on the back of your neck. It was a speech that you would appreciate much more on the battlefield or in a guerrilla camp than at your radio in a comfortable living room back home. I don't know how it sounded back in the United States, but it was not meant for the people back home. It was meant for the Filipino people and they really liked it. Their beloved leader was back. Now they could get ammunition, weapons, and medicines. Every guerrilla radio station in the Philippines was turned on that day and the results were apparent immediately. We got pledges for help and calls for instructions from all over the country. Give the Filipino a leader and something to fight with and he is an excellent ally, just as he is a dangerous enemy if he is on the other side.

MacArthur called on them to arise and strike. It was an emotional appeal to an emotional people. . . .

He then turned the microphone over to President Osmena.

There had been some talk about MacArthur's three top commanders, of land, sea, and air forces, following Osmena with statements, and Kinkaid had already prepared his speech. Neither Krueger nor I wanted to take part in the program. I felt that it was a sort of homecoming for MacArthur and President Osmena, and that, if anyone else followed him, it should be a Filipino. General MacArthur decided that if all three of us were not going to talk, none of us would. That was all right with me and I imagine it was with the others.

LIFE APPLAUDS THE SAVIOR OF THE PHILIPPINES (1945) [6]

"I shall return," said General Douglas MacArthur, fleeing Bataan in 1942. "I have returned," he said at Leyte Gulf, and last week he

[6] From General Douglas MacArthur, "Return to the Philippines," *Life Magazine*, 18 (February 19, 1945): 28. Copyright © 1945 by Time, Inc. Reprinted by permission of the publisher.

entered flaming, weeping Manila. When MacArthur hurls the cape of history over his shoulder, he often conceals as much drama as he makes. More than 40 years of American Far Eastern adventure lay behind that entrance; adventure more real to no American than to Douglas MacArthur himself.

His father, Arthur MacArthur, was a general in the U.S. Army that first occupied Manila in August 1898. His father saw Aguinaldo captured; as military governor he gave the first organized training to Filipino troops. To Douglas MacArthur, Manila is a home. There, ten years ago, he buried his mother; there he courted his wife. And there, his U.S. Military career seemingly over, he took an old man's job in 1936 as field marshal for the new Philippine Commonwealth, creating an army for his good friend Manuel Quezon.

When he was restored to active service in the U.S. Army in July 1941, he had six months to merge the U.S. and Philippine forces into one force for defense against the Jap. One force they were, all the way down Bataan. One force they remained during the dark three years of occupation, linked by jungle radios and an occasional submarine or plane. In the seams of their clothing the Filipino guerrillas treasured U.S. news leaflets with Douglas MacArthur's picture on them. For the Filipinos revere MacArthur and even credit him with superhuman powers. Who else could have diverted the expected typhoon before the landing on Leyte or reduced the surf at Lingayen Gulf to its lowest ebb in native memory? He brought Tommy guns of new designs; the Filipinos, never more than a few months behind Chicago in U.S. slang, dubbed them "Flash Gordons."

MacArthur's career spans all of U.S.-Philippine history. To Filipinos he owes the chance that has proved him a truly great general. And he is himself the culmination of an old island tradition: that Americans are supermen, the half-divine protectors and deliverers of William Howard Taft's "little brown brother."

21

Japan, Formosa, and the Korean War, 1945-1951

In the postwar years, MacArthur became a more controversial figure, as his frequently-expressed views on foreign policy issues increasingly diverged from those of the Truman Administration. The Cold War, of course, played a major role in dividing the followers of the general from those of the President. Judging from the remarks of George F. Kennan of the State Department's policy planning staff, MacArthur moved more slowly than Washington desired in adapting the Occupation of Japan to the Truman Administration's Cold War objectives. On the other hand, Major General Courtney Whitney, MacArthur's former aide and confidant, and Averell Harriman, a spokesman for the President, show just how far the rift had widened—with the sides reversed—in their evaluation of Chiang Kai-shek. The Korean War heightened differences of opinion between liberals and conservatives, and this is amply evidenced by the growing criticism and adulation of MacArthur. John Gunther's study of the general is one of the last attempts at a balanced assessment before MacArthur's dismissal from his commands split the nation into two hostile camps.

GEORGE F. KENNAN CRITICIZES THE OCCUPATION OF JAPAN [1]

It is with amazement and concern that I personally took note of this state of affairs in the summer of 1947. . . . If one was to regard the protection of Japan against Communist pressures as a legitimate concern of the United States government, then it was simply madness to think of abandoning Japan to her own devices in the situation then prevailing. She had been totally disarmed and demilitarized. After cession to the Soviet Union of southern Sakhalin and the Kurile Islands, and with the Russians in occupation of North Korea, she was semisurrounded by the military positions of the Soviet Union. Yet no provision of any sort had been made by the occupational regime for her future defense. . . . In addition to this, Japan's central police establishment had been destroyed. She had no effective means of com-

[1] From George F. Kennan, *Memoirs, 1925–1950* (Boston: Atlantic, Little, Brown and Company, 1967), pp. 375–76, 386–90. Copyright © 1967 by George F. Kennan. Reprinted by permission of the author and publisher.

batting the Communist penetration and political pressure that was already vigorously asserting itself under the occupation and could be depended upon to increase greatly if the occupation was removed and American forces withdrawn. In the face of this situation the nature of the occupational policies pursued up to that time by General Mac-Arthur's headquarters seemed on cursory examination to be such that if they had been devised for the specific purpose of rendering Japanese society vulnerable to Communist political pressures and paving the way for a Communist takeover, they could scarcely have been other than what they were. . . .

The picture that emerged from . . . study of the situation in Japan confirmed in full the anxieties we in the staff had experienced when we first inquired into the matter the previous autumn. In no respect was Japan at that time in a position to shoulder and to bear successfully the responsibilities of independence. . . .

It was true, in the first place, that no proper provision had been made for Japan's defense. SCAP had in Japan at that time a total of some 87,000 military personnel. Most of these were engaged in housekeeping duties. The most that could have been raised in the way of combat forces out of this number would have been one or two combat teams. The Japanese were themselves of course totally disarmed, and no one had any idea of rearming them.

Our occupational establishment was weighing heavily on Japanese life and preempting a good part of what was needed for economic recovery. . . . The occupation costs were absorbing approximately one-third of the Japanese budget. The cumbersome occupational establishment was in many respects parasitical; and I am sorry to say that among the various purposes for which exactions were being made upon the Japanese, the personal enrichment of members of the occupation was not always absent.

Saddled with such a burden it would have been difficult for the Japanese to prepare themselves for independence even in the best of circumstances. But in addition to this, the effect of the reforms which SCAP had been conducting, and of the manner in which it had been conducting them, was such as to produce just at that time a high degree of instability in Japanese life generally.

The land reform, in itself constructive and desirable, had affected about one-third of the arable land of the country and had led to the purchase by the Japanese government of a very large part of this property with a view to its redistribution. Only about one-seventh of what had been purchased had, however, been resold up to that point.

The result was a situation of great confusion and instability in the relationships of agricultural land ownership.

A similar situation existed on the industrial side. SCAP had embraced with an almost wild enthusiasm the trust-busting ideals that already commended themselves so powerfully to the antitrust division of the Department of Justice in Washington. Some two hundred and sixty Japanese companies, including some of the most tremendous industrial concerns, had been designated as "excessive concentrations of economic power." Their securities had in many instances been taken over by the Japanese government at SCAP's direction and were theoretically awaiting resale—to whom was not clear. The companies, meanwhile, existed in a state of uncertainty which could not help but interfere seriously with initiative and confidence of management. The ideological concepts on which these measures rested bore so close a resemblance to Soviet views about the evils of "capitalist monopolies" that the measures themselves could only have been eminently agreeable to anyone interested in the future communization of Japan. Their relation to the interests of Japanese recovery was less apparent.

Most serious of all, as I saw it, was the situation created by the wholesale "purging" of people in government, in education, and in business who were suspected of having had militaristic sympathies or of having abetted Japanese aggression in earlier days. Here SCAP had proceeded on a scale, and with a dogmatic, impersonal vindictiveness, for which there are few examples outside the totalitarian countries themselves. Seven hundred thousand people had already been involved, at the time of our visit, in the attendant screenings. Just in the educational establishment alone, some 120,000 out of a half million teachers had been purged or had resigned to avoid purging. Nor was there any visible end to this process. SCAP had decreed that checks should henceforth be run under its supervision on all new governmental employees, so this sort of screening was apparently intended to go on indefinitely. The program, furthermore, had taken on a wholly unfathomable complexity. Orders, regulations, and institutions relating to this process had been piled on top of each other in appalling confusion. . . . The indiscriminate purging of whole categories of individuals, sickeningly similar to totalitarian practices, was in conflict with the civil rights provisions of the new constitution that we ourselves had imposed upon the Japanese. . . . Important elements of Japanese society essential to its constructive development were being driven underground. . . . Particularly strange and unfortunate was the regularity with which the purge had seemed to hit persons known in the days before the war for their friendly attitude toward the United States. It was as though pro-Americanism, especially among upper-class Japanese, was particularly suspect. Here, again, the policies of SCAP had brought Japanese life to a point of great turmoil and confusion, and had produced, momentarily at least, a serious degree of instability.

Meanwhile, economic recovery was being further hampered by reparations deliveries, particularly of industrial equipment previously in use in Japan, to various allies—the Chinese, the Philippines, etc. Not only were these deliveries and the uncertainties connected with their possible continuation damaging the Japanese economy, but they were doing very little to strengthen anybody else's economy. Masses of this equipment lay rotting, we were told, on the docks at Shanghai and other Far Eastern ports.

Obviously, such conditions would constitute, in the event that the occupation should be suddenly removed, a high degree of vulnerability to Communist pressures. Yet nothing was being done to provide the Japanese with any adequate means of looking to their own internal security. The only police units under central control were some thirty thousand rural constabulary. The municipal police forces, amounting to some 77,000 men, were under only local control, with no provision for proper liaison among them or between them and the center in matters of political security; yet it was precisely here, in the cities, that the problem of Communist activity would be most acute. This whole establishment was armed, for the most part, only with pistols and of these there were less than one weapon to every four men. There was no counterintelligence force. Although Japan was an island country, no maritime police force had been created. And there was, of course, no Japanese armed force to back up any of these units in case of emergency. It was difficult to imagine a setup more favorable and inviting from the standpoint of the prospects for a Communist take-over. The Japanese Communists at the same time were being given a free field for political activity and were increasing their strength rapidly.

COURTNEY WHITNEY: THE GENERAL AND THE GENERALISSIMO [2]

In hindsight and in the United States it is simpler than it was at the time in Tokyo to see the animosity against MacArthur that was

[2] Excerpted from Courtney Whitney, *MacArthur: His Rendezvous with History* (New York: Alfred A. Knopf, 1956), pp. 368–69, 371–75, 383. Copyright © 1955 by Time, Inc. Reprinted by permission of the publisher.

rampant in Washington during the Korean war. But even reviewing and studying it today, I still find it difficult to understand. It seems clear that when President Truman, Secretaries Acheson and Johnson, and General Bradley met in the White House office and decided to go into the war, their intention at the outset was not to use American lives as pawns in lengthly bargaining sessions with the leaders of Asian Communism. I cannot believe—and neither can MacArthur—that these men plotted among themselves to kill 31,000 United States soldiers and spend 22 billion dollars only to ruin American prestige all over Asia.

But this was the actual result of the policies they adopted. Somehow their aims got twisted. Perhaps they were not thinking, but were only swinging blindly in the darkness of wishful ignorance when they struck back at the North Koreans in June 1950. Whatever their intention when they made their gesture of defiance, all Asia applauded. But then, when little by little America's posture turned from that of the powerful defender of the right to a timid appeasement of the wrong, Asian admiration turned to shocked disillusionment.

This MacArthur *could* see better from Tokyo than others could from Washington or Lake Success. But what surpassed his understanding was the reason why. It still does.

It took a little time for American courage and defiance of Communist aggression to become transformed into the kind of attitude that produced the losing stalemate at Panmunjon. But the signs of growing timidity in Washington were surprisingly fast in appearing, even ten thousand miles away in MacArthur's headquarters. The first clear indication he had that the United States might actually compromise with victory came in the handling of Formosa. MacArthur of course could not believe at first that the supposed leader of the world's nations would reverse all American history and adopt a foreign policy of vacillation and weakness. It took the strange Washington behavior over Formosa to suggest to him that this might unhappily be the fact. . . .

MacArthur was somewhat puzzled by all this. But he was even more puzzled by the many conflicting reports that were coming from Formosa and other sources on the subject of military capabilities of the island for defense. As in World War II and as in Korea, the only way he could get a clear picture of the situation was to go and have a look himself. He explained this to the Joint Chiefs and told them that he would proceed to Formosa on July 31 as planned.

The flight was uneventful, except for a delay at its destination, when bad weather kept us circling Taipei's airfield for an hour and a half while Generalissimo Chiang Kai-shek and the members of his government waited below. I was struck with the fact that after all these years of fighting Japanese and Communist aggression side by side, as it were, these two comrades-in-arms had never actually met. Now, as they shook hands, MacArthur said: "How do you do, Generalissimo? It was nice of you to come down and meet me."

With no more ado, they climbed into a sedan and set off for a military briefing and a conference with the chief Chinese Nationalist leader with whom MacArthur would have to deal in the joint defense of the island. It was a busy day, but at the end of it MacArthur felt that he had obtained a general "feel" not only of the local military situation but on such intelligence from the mainland as had come out through Nationalist channels.

That evening we were guests at a formal dinner given by Generalissimo and Madame Chiang Kai-shek at their home. The Generalissimo's natural handicap in his inability to speak English on such social occasions was more than made up by his wife's charm as a hostess. She personally greeted by name every guest as he arrived, though she had never met most of us and probably had only heard of us through an official briefing for the occasion; how she did it I do not know. She made everyone at once feel the warmth of the hospitality of this great leader and his wife, who for so long have symbolized implacable resistance to the advance of Communism in the Far East. . . .

It did not dawn on MacArthur that his visit to Formosa would be construed as being sinister in any way. The area in which he had military responsibility had been enlarged by the President so as to include Formosa, and MacArthur was accordingly attempting to make his own military estimate of the situation. But in order to forestall in advance any criticism that his trip had been other than military, he issued the following statement as soon as he returned to Tokyo:

"My visit to Formosa has been primarily for the purpose of making a short reconnaissance of the potentiality of its defenses against possible attack. . . . Arrangements have been completed for effective coordination between the American forces under my command and those of the Chinese Government, the better to meet any attack which a hostile force might be foolish enough to attempt. Such an attack would, in my opinion, stand little chance of success. It has been a great pleasure for me to meet my old comrade-in-arms of the last war, Generalissimo Chiang Kai-shek. His indomitable determination to resist Communist domination arouses my sincere admiration. His determination parallels the common interests and purpose of Americans, that all people in the Pacific area shall be free—not slaves."

But despite his clear statement that it was a military and not a political trip, the cry immediately went up that MacArthur and Chiang Kai-shek had been plotting some kind of international deviltry at their meeting. It was not surprising that the Communist press and their fellow travelers erupted in screams of outrage over MacArthur's eulogy of the Generalissimo's resistance to Communism. For a few days there was a frenzy of irresponsible diatribe, but soon the Communist switch was pulled. As usual, the pack took off in some other direction.

What was surprising, however, was to hear echoes of this cry from the U.S. State Department. . . .

By August 10 some of the misrepresentations had become so gross and obviously malicious that they were causing world-wide reaction. The situation seemed to be rapidly getting out of hand, and yet no attempt was being made in Washington even to answer some of the outright lies which were greatly disturbing many of the other U.N. governments.

In fact, some of the misrepresentations appeared to have been encouraged by various government officials in Washington. At least one reporter was flatly told, for example, that MacArthur had not even notified the President before he went to Formosa. As I have already pointed out, there was a considerable exchange of messages on the subject. Whether the Joint Chiefs of Staff, with whom it was MacArthur's responsibility to communicate, passed this important information to the White House or not, MacArthur could hardly know. But to leave Tokyo for whatever destination at so important a time without informing Washington would be unthinkable to MacArthur. It is difficult to conceive of the Joint Chiefs of Staff neglecting to tell the President that MacArthur had notified them of his intention to visit the island.

One can only guess at where in Washington the slip-up occurred, but a logical conjecture might be that there was no slip-up at all—that the Joint Chiefs believed that the State Department would inform Truman and that the responsible State Department official purposely kept it from the President in order further to embarrass MacArthur. Aside from gross negligence on the part of both Joint Chiefs of Staff and the State Department, the only alternative answer to the mystery is the improbable one that the President himself, or a White

House official close to him, was intentionally lying in accusing Mac-Arthur of not informing Washington ahead of time. . . .

But the pressure to betray our Nationalist Allies of World War II has never let up; it has, in fact, increased over the years. It started right after the war's end, when pseudo "liberals" argued that the Chinese Communists were really only "agrarian reformers"—a claim that has become one of modern history's bitterest jests. It was of course given its greatest impetus when General Marshall made the tragic mistake of using American prestige as a lever for forcing a "coalition government" on Chiang Kai-shek. And it manifested itself most vocally when MacArthur tried to implement the President's directive to defend Formosa by strengthening the alliance between Nationalist and U.S. military forces.

The arguments of this cynical school of thought have taken many forms. At first the claim was that Chiang's government was corrupt. Somehow the reasoning ran that rule by the Kuomintang was even worse than a Communist police state, and that therefore any change would be for the better. Who these people were, especially in the U.S. State Department, who would ally with the same Chiang against the Japanese but not against the Communists, was never clear. This wishful foolishness has been aided and abetted mostly by the British, especially by leaders of England's Labour Party, who have even toured Red China and written eulogizing books and articles about the new slave state.

In any event it has always been MacArthur's fervent hope that no such casuistry will long beguile American political leaders. As this is written, the United States is paying the price of the specious reasoning that compromise and timidity will fool the Asian Communists. Had the President—as well as his political advisers playing strategists and his military advisers playing politics—listened to the clear and simple warning of MacArthur five years ago, we would not today be frantically trying to stem the rush of Communism, directed against Indochina, Indonesia, Burma, and especially Formosa, that key island of our own defense system. . . .

AVERELL HARRIMAN MEETS THE GENERAL (1950) [8]

In my first talk with MacArthur, I told him the President wanted me to tell him he must not permit Chiang to be the cause of

[8] Reprinted by permission of W. Averell Harriman.

starting a war with the Chinese communists on the mainland, the effect of which might drag us into a world war. . . .

For reasons which are rather difficult to explain, I did not feel that we came to a full agreement on the way we believe things should be handled on Formosa and with the Generalissimo. He accepted the President's position and will act accordingly, but without full conviction. He has a strange idea that we should back anybody who will fight communism, even though he could not give an argument why the Generalissimo's fighting communists would be a contribution towards the effective dealing with the communists in China. I pointed out to him the basic conflict of interest between the U.S. and the Generalissimo's position as to the future of Formosa, namely, the preventing of Formosa's falling into hostile hands. . . . Chiang, on the other hand, had only the burning ambition to use Formosa as a stepping-stone for his re-entry to the mainland. MacArthur recognized that this ambition could not be fulfilled, and yet thought it might be a good idea to let him land. . . . He did not seem to consider the liability that our support of Chiang on such a move would be to us in the East. I explained in great detail why Chiang was a liability, and the great danger of a split in the unity of the United Nations on the Chinese-Communist-Formosa policies. . . .

MacArthur would never recognize the Chinese Communists, even to the use of the veto in seating the Communists. . . . We should be more aggressive than we have been so far in creating stronger dissension within China. . . .

In all, I cannot say that he recognizes fully the difficulties, both within the world and within the East, of whatever moves we make within China in our position with the Generalissimo in Formosa. He believes that our policies undermine the Generalissimo. . . .

MacArthur feels that we have not improved our position by kicking Chiang around, and hoped that the President would do something to relieve the strain that existed between the State Department and the Generalissimo. He suggested the President might reiterate his previous statements by threatening the Chinese Communists that he would withdraw the inhibition to attack the airfields on the mainland if the Chinese continued to do this work, or build up their positions. I told him that if he wanted to make that recommendation to the President it was up to him, but I assured him that I would strongly recommend to the President against his doing so. I emphasized the overpowering importance of UN unity and that this would give further trouble and give the Russians a chance to develop an entering wedge.

HAROLD L. ICKES: "MACARTHUR TALKS TOO MUCH" (1950)[4]

No American would be so blind to the facts or so prejudiced as to deny that, on more than one occasion, General MacArthur has shown real flashes of genius as a field commander. But he talks too much. It is one thing for a general to encourage his troops so that their morale may be high on the eve of an impending battle. But it is quite another thing to tell the world in advance that a certain objective will be attained within a given time, or that a battle is about to be undertaken that will end all battles in the war being waged.

Nor should a general play politics or try to usurp from the President the conduct of foreign affairs. MacArthur has done both. To begin with, he was MacArthur the Un-ready when the North Koreans invaded South Korea. Fortunately for him, it was possible to stabilize the UN line with the aid of the Navy and the Air Force. A brilliant and daring landing was made well beyond the North Korean line. Seoul was recaptured and hundreds of thousands of North Korean troops were apparently surrounded. The remnants of the North Korean army was driven north of the 38th Parallel. The army of the UN achieved its original objective which was to clear South Korea of enemies.

At this point, many Americans felt that there should be a carefully-considered definition of our final objective. They believed that the UN should call upon all Koreans to compose their difficulties, and if they failed to do so Pandit Nehru of India should be asked to mediate the differences between the belligerents. But apparently MacArthur, saturated with self-esteem, as usual, and exalted by the clackings of political partisans of the minuscule mentality of Harold E. Stassen and Joseph R. McCarthy, saw an opportunity to destroy Communism via China and thus become the greatest military hero that the world had ever seen. Why should "The MacArthur" demean himself by asking for orders or by deferring to inferior men who, by accident, happened to outrank him?

MacArthur's troops, excepting only those of South Korea, were held briefly south of the 38th Parallel, but the South Koreans, either on their own or under the encouragement of MacArthur, pushed across the important Parallel in pursuit of North Korean troops who, after

[4] From Harold Ickes, "MacArthur Talks Too Much," *The New Republic,* 123 (December 11, 1950): 18. Copyright © 1950 by Harrison-Blaine of New Jersey, Inc. Reprinted by permission of the publisher.

all, had not been bottled up south of Seoul. At the time when the diplomats should have taken over, Acheson hesitated, and MacArthur brazenly began to exercise political power in the Far East. It was another instance of filling a vacuum. Without waiting for the UN and without even consulting his Commander-in-Chief, the President, who alone under our Constitution has the power to conduct foreign relations, MacArthur flew to Formosa to kiss the hand of Mme. Chiang Kai-shek. Following this, American supplies, unauthorized by Washington, began to flow to the grafting and corrupt Nationalistic Junta that holds Formosa by the strength of the American fleet.

When this news began to leak and Communist China became alarmed as to the ultimate designs of MacArthur, Truman made the dangerous trip to Wake Island to tell the over-weening MacArthur that the conduct of diplomatic affairs still belonged to the President. Instead of running the risk of the flight to Wake Island, President Truman should have replaced MacArthur with a more responsible general such as Eisenhower who, like MacArthur, knows how to fight but who has the additional virtue of knowing when not to talk. But a tough political fight was on, and reckless Republicans demanded that the President, not a Republican, strip himself of his Constitutional power to conduct foreign affairs in favor of MacArthur, a self-conscious Republican.

As this is being written, MacArthur's chickens have been coming home to roost. The United States faces a deadlier peril than at the time of Pearl Harbor. Insubordinately, MacArthur, despite outspoken warnings from Communist China, had been deliberately inching not only the United States but the United Nations forward into a war that did not have to be fought and from which we could not hope to disentangle ourselves for an unpredictable period. Establishment of a neutral zone in Korea might have prevented war.

Of course, MacArthur and his hobbledygee sycophants who have been thrusting knives into the United States Constitution will try to place the blame elsewhere—where it does not belong. In fact, MacArthur is already doing so. Since the disaster in North Korea that MacArthur kept asking for, he discovered that his good clean funning, consisting of "comments passed between my field commanders and myself in a jocular vein" had been "exaggerated" into a prediction that "the boys will be home from Korea by Christmas." It may take MacArthur a long time to set the "exaggeration" straight.

If we become deeply involved in a war with Communist China, as seems to be in prospect, it will cost America and the world more than we can afford. It will postpone world peace indefinitely, perhaps finally. MacArthur calls it "a new war." He ought to know.

JOHN GUNTHER ANALYZES MACARTHUR'S CHARACTER (1951)[5]

His dominating characteristic, next to courage, is probably ego. Out of this ego, which is measureless, come some of his most useful characteristics, like confidence, magnetism, and the capacity to inspire utter devotion in his followers. Out of it, too, come some negative traits like his touchiness and sensitiveness to criticism, which is accentuated by the extreme touchiness of his staff. Also he has a conspicuous tendency to reward loyalty too much for its own sake—to count too much on old comrades in arms who have grown with him during the years. There should be newer blood around MacArthur. But he will not tolerate anybody near him being too big. I even heard it said, "None of MacArthur's men can *risk* being first-rate."

There is such a thing as a man being so vain that he is not vain. To pretend to have no vanity is the greatest of all vanities. MacArthur's ego is, in a way, of this special type. Everybody knows about the tilt of his gilt-edged cap, the carefully pressed uniforms and shining boots, the open-throated profile flung at cameras. The General has terrific style. If, in the abstract, you set out to draw a picture of the quintessentially ideal commander, the perfect type of composite soldier-hero, it might turn out to be astonishingly like MacArthur. Even the fact that he unostentatiously wears *no* decorations whatever is part of his ostentation. But his peacockry is more than merely a surface matter. Once he said to an interviewer (perhaps with tongue in cheek) that his major advisors were—Washington and Lincoln!

An eminent officer of World War I, General Enoch Crowder, once told a high official of the State Department, "I thought that Arthur MacArthur [the General's father] was the most flamboyantly egotistic man I had ever seen—until I met his son."

Just before the Korean war MacArthur had plenty of things on his mind but he found time to send a visitor to Tokyo, with the request that it be returned, a postcard he had just had from India. He thought the visitor might be amused by this example of his fan mail, and moreover he wanted to keep it. The address on the postcard was:

[5] From John Gunther, *The Riddle of MacArthur: Japan, Korea and the Far East* (New York: Harper & Row, Publishers, 1951), pp. 23–29. Copyright © 1950 by John Gunther. Reprinted by permission of the publisher.

To His Most Gracious Majesty
The Old Friend
The Most Honorable
General MacArthur, Sahib, Bahadur,
Military Governor and Crowned King of Japan

Perhaps it is his sense of duty that makes MacArthur egotistic. He can be—and often is—relaxed, gay, and even shy. He carries the plumage of a flamingo, but his voice can be modest too. By no means is he always stern, pontifical, defiant. He is, in fact, almost as notable a winner-over of the reluctant as Roosevelt; persuasiveness is one of his paramount qualities. Consider what a tremendous impression he is apt to make on a casual visitor; then estimate how magnetic he must be to people close by. Still, few people outside his immediate entourage really *like* him. They may respect him, admire him, emulate him, or even worship him (as many Japanese and Filipinos undoubtedly do) but it is hard to imagine him as a universal mass leader, at least so far as the rank and file of the American public are concerned. MacArthur is a Caesar, and not, let us say, a man overwhelmingly beloved like Gandhi.

But by his own men, the rockfast inner circle, he is adulated. Tokyo is full of retired oldsters who practically stand on street corners to tell you with pride how intimate they are with him even if they haven't laid eyes on him for a year. I have heard him seriously compared to Alexander the Great by a member of his staff, to Alexander's disadvantage. Another officer told me with absolute seriousness that he considered MacArthur to be the greatest man who ever lived.

His entourage, probably without his direct knowledge, goes to interesting lengths to perform various subtle—and sometimes not so subtle—maneuvers for augmentation of his prestige. After the communist attack on Korea, the word was quietly passed around that it was solely MacArthur's vigorous intervention in Washington which led Mr. Truman to announce that the United States would give military assistance to the South Korean government. A few days later, the "line" switched, and primary credit was passed on to Mr. Johnson, who was then Secretary of Defense. The reason was that the military news was bad and MacArthur's men did not want the Supreme Commander to be held responsible in case the Korean adventure continued to go wrong.

Another MacArthur trait is his signal tendency to overoptimism and wishful thinking, a characteristic which has led him to errors of judgment and blunders on occasion. For instance he did genuinely think in the late 1930's that the Philippines, given time, could successfully defend themselves against Japan. And—to come up to date—he most distinctly did *not* anticipate major Chinese intervention in Korea in 1950, though he had sounded noisy warnings about how dangerous the situation was. He is, most people in Tokyo believe, far from realistic about the future course of Japanese affairs. MacArthur wants desperately to believe that the democratization of Japan will progress and stick, if only because this would be his own supreme accomplishment. But how much of the SCAP reformation will endure no man can know.

MacArthur's positive qualities and merits are, of course, many. For one thing, he is packed with brains. For another, let nobody underestimate his sheer, immense force of character. An American officer who was a cadet when he was superintendent of West Point was asked his opinion of the General. Reply: "He's the only man in the world who could walk into a room full of drunks and all would be stone sober within five minutes."

His memory is photographic, and he is blessed with one of the most useful advantages that mortal man can possess—he reads very quickly. He has a profound knowledge of military history, and loves to quote from old historians. The story has been told that he got the idea for the Inchon landing by rereading accounts of Wolfe's campaign against Quebec in 1759. Apparently he never forgets *anything*. It is only a minor sidelight, but it certainly impressed me that in Tokyo in 1950 he recalled vividly and accurately some details of a conversation I had with him in Manila in 1938. Once he was discussing proposals to modify the original plans for the American invasion of Honshu, the main island of Japan. On his own authority MacArthur was working over the directives that had been sent him from Washington, and he wanted to land in a different place, north of Tokyo. Someone pointed out that the surf along that particular stretch of beach was apt to be nasty. "Certainly," the General said. "I remember seeing it when I came out to Japan with my father in 1905."

Dennis McEvoy, the representative in Tokyo of the *Reader's Digest,* presented his wife to the Supreme Commander some time ago. MacArthur began to reminisce about a prize fight he had seen in company with her grandfather, M. H. De Young, in San Francisco *forty-seven* years before. The General remembered who had won the fight, who had fought in the semifinals, and what other guests were in the party.

He has a pleasant and ready wit. At lunch in Tokyo, when he happened to be talking about the Prince of Wales, I asked him if he had seen an article in *Life* wherein the Duke of Windsor describes a golf match he had played with Emperor Hirohito in the 1920's. Both these regal figures were crown princes then. It became clear to the Prince of Wales that Hirohito had never had a golf club in his hand before, and so the Prince politely pretended that he too could not hit the ball. MacArthur laughed and then seized the point at once. "How pleasant that two men destined to be heads of state should be gentlemen with each other!"

His tact is marked. For instance, when he receives the Emperor today, only one interpreter is present, and it is always an interpreter whom the Emperor brings, not MacArthur's. Though nicely sensitive to the personality of visitors, he never agrees just for the sake of amiability, as Roosevelt did. He loves to talk, loves an audience, and loves applause.

That he talks a great deal—and eloquently—is famous. I have seldom met anybody who gives such a sense of the richness and flexibility of the English language; he draws out of it—like Winston Churchill—as out of some inexhaustible reservoir. His manner of delivery is somewhat jerky; his choice of words, again as with Mr. Churchill, is often archaic. Of course, like many great talkers, he never stops; he is an old-fashioned monologist par excellence. Sometimes he is so bewitched by his own eloquence that he forgets what he has just said. Recently he received a group of American friends at a lunch that lasted from two to five, and he hardly stopped talking once. At one point he told an anecdote about La Rochefoucauld. Twenty minutes later he told the identical anecdote, having already forgotten that he had just told it.

General Eisenhower called on him in Tokyo during the period when both men were being conspicuously mentioned for the Presidency. Eisenhower was before the war a junior member of MacArthur's staff in Manila. The two generals respect one another heartily. In Tokyo, however, members of the MacArthur entourage are blindly, savagely jealous of Eisenhower and his political prestige and popularity. Eisenhower could not get a word in for three quarters of an hour, while MacArthur reminisced about old times. Then Eisenhower interrupted to say, with emphasis and much elaboration, that he did not think that any military man should be President of the United States. His sincerity was manifest. But MacArthur cocked a wary eye at him and said, "That's the way to play it, Ike."

It is astonishing that anybody who talks as well as MacArthur should write so badly. Perhaps the Supreme Commander is not responsible for some of his more reedy speeches and the rodomontade he customarily employs. It is not merely that his style is pompous. It is worse than that. Once he replied to a congratulatory telegram from an admiral with the words, "May God protect and preserve them [the admiral's sailors] is my prayer from Tokyo as the world keeps turning over and over and over."

One of MacArthur's secrets is his sense of balance, as in all just men. He is a man of no softness whatever, but he likes to see both sides. The leader of a Japanese delegation that visited the United States recently was much struck when the General told him, "Look for the bad things too."

He has, like all competent executives, a capacity to seize things quickly and apparently by intuition. One of his close associates told me, "He only gets what *we* give him—how then does he always know so much more than we do? He is never wrong. If a junior officer is about to be invalided home, he knows about it before we tell him. How does he *know?*"

He throws himself into whatever task he has with complete absorption, he has inflexible belief in his own destiny, and he has the compulsive ego of the truly dedicated.

Finally, one of MacArthur's dominant qualities is the master quality of courage. His physical courage is legendary; it is quite safe to say that no general officer in modern history, let alone a theater commander, ever took such risks. Time and again, in both world wars, he has exposed himself to brutal fire in a manner reckless—but casual —almost beyond belief. He never wears a steel helmet, and seldom carries arms. He stalks a battlefront like a man hardly human, not only arrogantly but lazily. The attitude is Napoleonic; the bullet that will strike him has not yet been cast. He was called "Dugout Doug" by disgruntled sailors, marines, and G.I.'s in the Pacific; the accusation that he ever hid from anything is just plain silly. Japan is a country notorious (until recently at least) for its addiction to political assassination; but MacArthur never takes any but the most primitive precautions. He enters and leaves the Dai-Ichi four times a day, every day of the year, and invariably a crowd of from fifty to a hundred Japanese assembles by the doorway to watch him. Traffic is not permitted on the streets while he moves, and an elevator is held for him within the building, but the crowd itself is not watched, and MacArthur is never (nowadays) accompanied by a guard of any kind. Any crank could throw a bomb or grenade. He pays no attention.

22
MacArthur's Dismissal (1951)

Truman's dismissal of MacArthur from his commands on April 11, 1951 touched off an uproar—largely favoring the general. A Gallup poll taken one week later found that only twenty-nine percent of the respondents approved of the President's decision, while sixty-two percent opposed it. Liberals strongly backed the President, but their voices were barely audible in the din stirred up by conservative Republicans. On April 12, Senator Joseph R. McCarthy charged that "treason in the White House" had been accomplished by "bourbon and benedictine" in the hands of men who knew how "to get the President cheerful." He concluded: "The s.o.b. should be impeached." Newspapers, news magazines, and church groups divided roughly along liberal and conservative lines, although Truman fared better in many editorial columns than he ordinarily did. MacArthur's tremendous popularity skewed much of the debate to the Right. The GOP seized upon the MacArthur issue to denounce the Truman Administration in the most violent terms, while the President's defenders often weakly replied that the dismissal of a general was within the powers of a Commander-in-Chief. MacArthur did not receive a fraction of the abuse heaped upon Truman. In the end, Truman did not win the debate; he merely weathered the storm.

TRUMAN RELIEVES MACARTHUR OF HIS COMMANDS [1]

With deep regret I have concluded that General of the Army Douglas MacArthur is unable to give his wholehearted support to the policies of the United States Government and of the United Nations in matters pertaining to his official duties. In view of the specific responsibilities imposed upon me by the Constitution of the United States and the added responsibility which has been entrusted to me by the United Nations, I have decided that I must make a change of command in the Far East. I have, therefore, relieved General MacArthur of his commands and have designated Lt. Gen. Matthew B. Ridgway as his successor.

[1] From *Public Papers of the Presidents of the United States: Harry S. Truman, Containing the Public Messages, Speeches, and Statements of the President, January 1 to December 31, 1951* (Washington, D.C.: United States Government Printing Office, 1965): 222.

Full and vigorous debate on matters of national policy is a vital element in the constitutional system of our free democracy. It is fundamental, however, that military commanders must be governed by the policies and directives issued to them in the manner provided by our laws and Constitution. In time of crisis, this consideration is particularly compelling.

General MacArthur's place in history as one of our greatest commanders is fully established. The Nation owes him a debt of gratitude for the distinguished and exceptional service which he has rendered his country in posts of great responsibility. For that reason I repeat my regret at the necessity for the action I feel compelled to take in his case.

CONGRESS

Senator Joseph R. McCarthy[2]

The discharge of MacArthur was the greatest victory for British diplomacy since the end of World War II.

I am not going to discuss this man Attlee, who temporarily heads the British Government, but I would like to introduce . . . a photostat of a letter written by Attlee, or part of a letter, in his own handwriting. It is extremely interesting, when we realize that Truman is the President of this country in name only, that the real President who discharged MacArthur is a rather sinister monster of many heads and many tentacles, a monster conceived in the Kremlin, and then given birth to by Acheson, with Attlee and Morrison as the midwives, and then nurtured into Frankenstein proportions by the Hiss crowd, who still run the State Department. . . . Let me read the closing lines of this letter of Attlee's written to a Communist group. He says:

I shall try to tell—

Mr. President, listen to the next words:

our comrades—

That is not an English word; it is not an American word. It is a Communist phrase for "member of the party." He says:

I shall try to tell our comrades at home what I have seen.

[2] U.S. Senate, 82nd Cong., 1st sess., *Congressional Record,* 97, Part 3, pp. 4261, 4267.

In the closing line we find the Communist slogan, "Workers of the world unite." Signed, "C. A. Attlee." . . .

It was in late 1937 or early 1938, so there is nothing new about Mr. Attlee's connection. He may have reformed, I do not know. . . . It is of interest to us when we realize that not Mr. Truman but Mr. Acheson, with advice from Mr. Attlee and Mr. Morrison, and with the aid of the Kremlin, have succeeded in sacking one of the greatest Americans I think that was ever born, and one of the greatest military leaders since long before the days of Genghis Khan. . . .

. . . People who are not for America, but who are for international communism—the pals of Alger Hiss, the espionage agent, the man who drafted the Yalta Agreement—are still running the State Department.

Senator William Knowland [3]

Mao Tse-tung in Peking and Josef Stalin in Moscow must have received great satisfaction at the action taken by the President of the United States in removing Gen. Douglas MacArthur from his position.

General MacArthur was a rock of Gibraltar against the further spread of communism in the East.

I invite the attention of the Senate to a story printed in this morning's New York *Times* by Mr. Walter H. Waggoner, stating that Great Britain has requested of the State Department of the United States that Red China be consulted on a Japanese peace treaty, and that, ultimately, if not now, the island of Formosa be turned over to Chinese Communists.

Mr. President, I do not know that my voice will carry as far as Formosa, but for the 8,000,000 free people on that island I wish to say that the groups which have been willing to sacrifice General MacArthur in Europe and in the United States will not hesitate to sacrifice the human liberties of 8,000,000 persons on the island of Formosa. They had better place their faith in the Lord and in their own strong right arm in order to defend their liberties from the betrayal which is in the making.

Mr. President, this morning I issued a brief statement which I wish to read into the RECORD:

> By his action the President has yielded to British and American critics of General MacArthur. Our position in Japan and the whole

[3] From U.S. Senate, 82nd Cong., 1st sess., *Congressional Record*, 97, Part 3, p. 3623.

Far East is placed in jeopardy by an action which most observers will interpret as a preliminary step to a far-eastern Munich. It is also a great victory for Secretary of State Acheson and his far-eastern policies. When General MacArthur arrives home the American people will have the opportunity to demonstrate to the world and to the President the high regard they have for MacArthur and his service to his country.

Mr. President, I predict that all over this land in every community in which General MacArthur may stop there will be such an outpouring that not even the White House will be able to misinterpret the sentiments of the American people.

Senator Richard M. Nixon[4]

Mr. Nixon submitted the following resolution (S. Res. 126), which was referred to the Committee on Armed Services:

Whereas the overwhelming majority of the American people are shocked, disheartened, and angered over the removal of General of the Army Douglas MacArthur from his posts of command in the Far East by action of the President of the United States; and

Whereas the strength and morale of the Armed Forces of the United States now engaged in the defense of the Nation against our enemies have been tragically weakened by this action of the President; and

Whereas the removal of General MacArthur from his posts of command reflects a policy of appeasement of the enemies of the United States: Therefore, be it

Resolved, That it is the sense of the Senate that the President of the United States has not acted in the best interests of the American people in relieving of his commands and depriving the United States of the services of General of the Army Douglas MacArthur and that the President should reconsider his action and should restore General MacArthur to the commands from which he was removed.

Senator William Jenner[5]

The only question is whether we were fighting in Korea to win. MacArthur told us the only way we could win was with more manpower. That was a military issue. Our Government was planning to send additional troops to Europe, where there was no fighting, and

---

[4] From U.S. Senate, 82nd Cong., 1st sess., *Congressional Record*, 97, Part 3, p. 3614.

[5] From U.S. Senate, 82nd Cong., 1st sess., *Congressional Record*, 97, Part 3, pp. 3618–19.

leave the men in Korea to fight a war of attrition with no hope of victory.

The administration refused even to work with the 2,000,000 fighting men from South Korea and Free China, who begged to fight against the Communists.

The American people have the right to know what are the military issues. Congress has the right to know what are the military issues. Statements of fact on the question of American security are entirely proper communications from a general in the field, to the American people.

Who wants to hide the facts? Who wants us not to win in Korea? Who wants a long-drawn-out war of attrition in which thousands more of American soldiers are killed to no purpose?

That is the question which Congress must answer.

This is another Pearl Harbor. Once again the military situation is used to cover up the political chicanery of the palace guard. They are planning something devious, we don't know what. Our allies know, but Congress does not. The administration kow-towed to our allies. England announces that Red China must be represented in the Japanese peace settlement, and must be given Formosa. Are we going along in a phony peace move in which we will surrender to the Communists everything for which our men have died? Meanwhile the men in the Politburo are watching every move we make. We dare not make the smallest mistake.

Congress cannot wait until years have passed to find out what is hidden beneath the confusion. Congress must find out now.

This is no Republican victory. Republicans cannot rejoice at a political advantage which means our country is in danger.

This issue is not for the Republicans in Congress but for all true Americans in Congress. We are not being governed by the Democratic Party. We are not being governed by the Fair Deal. I charge that this country today is in the hands of a secret inner coterie which is directed by agents of the Soviet Union. They have formed a popular front government like that in France in the thirties and we know how France was taken from within.

We have asked the President to dismiss Secretary Acheson, who would not turn his back on Communist agents in the State Department. We have asked the President to dismiss General Marshall who was the tool of Soviet agents in his betrayal of China and loss of our allies in Asia.

It is too late now for such minor remedies. We must cut this whole cancerous conspiracy out of our Government at once. Our only choice is to impeach President Truman and find out who is the secret invisible government which has so cleverly led our country down the road to destruction.

[Manifestations of applause in the galleries.]

Senator Kenneth S. Wherry[6]

To charge General MacArthur with attempting to involve the United States in a gigantic war with Red China and precipitate unleashing of a third world war is resented by every thinking American familiar with the glorious record of this great statesman, soldier, patriot.

The pygmies cannot bring down this giant, this tower of strength and deserving idol of the American people.

Compare the monumental record of General MacArthur with that of his accusers, with their record of moral decay, greed, corruption, and confusion of these weaklings in the Truman administration.

The result of such a comparison can be only an alarm to the American people.

With all the force that is in me, fellow Americans, I ask you to remember the admonition that "eternal vigilance is the price of liberty."

The obvious truth is that the ship of state is floundering in a whirlpool of mink coats, paternalism, RFC-influenced loans, crooked political machines in league with national organizations, class arrayed against class, and a new scandal the order of the day.

Yes, fellow Americans, it is high time to become vigilant and militant. Your freedoms are at stake, and there is danger that runaway inflation will consume the people's wealth and render our beloved country unable to stand as the bulwark of freedom against the communistic threat. . . .

I have seen no statements by General MacArthur that he wants a third world war. I have not seen any statement by him that he wants to send American foot soldiers into Manchuria. Certainly he has not suggested an all-out war with China. He has advised, that the offer of a half-million anti-Communist Chinese on Formosa to join the United Nations forces should be accepted.

Is there any reason why these volunteers should be rejected? They will take the places of thousands of American boys who will be drafted and sent to Korea.

[6] From U.S. 82nd Cong., 1st sess., *Appendix to the Congressional Record*, 97, p. A2028.

The North Korea Communists have no qualm against accepting the aid of any Communists, whether they be Chinese, Japanese, or Russian.

These anti-Communist Chinese on Formosa are directly interested in victory for the republican forces of Korea. They desire to aid the South Koreans. Why should their request for an opportunity to help be denied? Is it better to let your sons fight and die in Korea than to let these anti-Communist Chinese fight for a toehold toward eventual liberation of their native China?

But, yet, fellow Americans, that is what the administration's policy means. . . .

. . . The American people want to hear General MacArthur. They believe that from his vast knowledge and experience in the South Pacific, he can recommend a better way to accomplish vindication for the forces of freedom in Korea.

There is much more to this desperate situation than the mechanics of warfare. The attitude of Western Europe is obvious to the American people. It is quite natural that Western Europe would like to have priority on America's manpower and America's resources.

Why, the Socialist Government of Great Britain, which has not hesitated to permit the sale of war materials to Soviet Russia and Red China, and which has conducted a thriving business with the Communists through Hong Kong, now has the audacity to insist that Formosa be turned over to Red China and that Red China, the Moscow-directed bandits that took over the Republic of China, should sit with the United States in making a peace treaty with Japan.

The pattern is familiar. Step by step the Dean Acheson policy of appeasement of the Communists goes forward. There is rejoicing tonight among the pro-Communists who run in and out of the State Department like water through a sieve.

Congressman Ralph W. Gwinn[7]

MacArthur has been busted out with Wedemeyer, Chennault, Hurley, Denfeld, and Cromelin, because our own popular-front Communist-dominated Government does not really want to win the war in Korea. It refuses to answer MacArthur's questions on that point. He has asked for the help of the 2,000,000 men now in China and Korea. He asked for the help of the Japanese. Our Government refused. It would not even feed and supply 400,000 reservists now in

[7] From U.S. 82nd Cong., 1st sess., *Appendix to the Congressional Record*, 97, p. A1978.

training camps in Korea to relieve the pressure on our own boys, fighting and dying in Korea.

Thus the program mapped out by Alger Hiss and Owen Lattimore in 1945 to deliver the Asiatic people to godless communism is working out according to plan. They destroyed Chiang Kai-shek and his forces. They are determined to destroy Syngman Rhee and leave him no organized forces against communism.

Now with MacArthur out of the way Red China can be added to the family of nations and Formosa delivered to it. What is more with MacArthur out of Japan the floodgates are open to the organization of the Communist Party there. The Japanese people who made such a magnificent recovery under MacArthur—in fact all of the forces of freedom, have been let down into what looks like a red sea surrounding the whole of Asia.

This conduct of our foreign affairs in Asia and the refusal to give MacArthur help throws light on the European situation. We are sending ground forces to Europe to fight unequal ground forces from Russia. The commander in chief of these forces in Europe speaks freely as a military and political leader on both military and political subjects without censure. MacArthur confined his remarks to military affairs and was busted for that alone. Will our popular-front Communist-dominated Government in European policy deliver our forces in Europe to Moscow in the same way it has delivered them in Asia? This is the terrifying question growing out of the MacArthur incident.

Possibly nothing short of the setting of the stage for impeachment proceedings will bring out the tragic corruption in the management of our foreign affairs. It greatly exceeds our domestic corruption and its consequences are more damaging. Out of such a proceeding the people might organize an honest Government and offset the notion in the Kremlin that America will not fight communism at home, in Asia or in Europe.

It is depressing beyond words that the Communist-dominated government in Britain was ready to blast the news, almost before we got it, that the victory had been won—MacArthur was out—Red China would be recognized and Formosa delivered to it.

Senator Hubert H. Humphrey[8]

The real issue involved in the President's dismissal of General MacArthur is one basic to American Constitutional Government. The

[8] From U.S. 82nd Cong., 1st sess., *Appendix to the Congressional Record*, 97, pp. A2306–A2307.

President, under the mandate of our Constitution, is Commander in Chief. The President, under the political tradition of our Republic, is responsible for foreign policy. It has been a basic principle of representative government that the military is subordinate to the civilian. The military officers and services are the servants of the Republic, not the master. The action of the President is within the tradition of American Constitutional Government. . . .

General MacArthur, as an individual, has a perfect right to disagree with our Government's foreign policy, but as a general subordinate to his Commander in Chief, he has neither the right nor the prerogative to formulate and attempt to carry out his own program and to disregard the program established by the Government. While I have a high regard for General MacArthur and his abilities, I am not prepared to accept his judgment over that of the President, the Secretary of State, the overwhelming majority of the representatives in the United Nations, the majority in the Congress, the Secretary of Defense, and the combined Chiefs of Staff. It should be clearly recognized that the bold statements of General MacArthur were causing great concern in other nations and among our allies.

While it is true that we as a Nation have been bearing the major burden of the war in Korea, we do have allies there, and those allies stand with us in Western Europe. They are the only allies that we have. It is impossible to keep allies and to maintain a solid defense against Communist aggression if we as a Nation and a Government act in opposition to our allies and disregard their wishes, their policies, and their program. To put it quite bluntly, faced as we are by the Soviet Union and its satellites, with a total population of over 800,000,000, we cannot afford to stand alone. The Soviet Union is doing everything in its power to break us away from our allies. The old tactic of divide and conquer is again being utilized. We must not fall prey to this tactic. We must stand together and work together.

The issue of foreign policy which divides us today is primarily related to our country's relations with Red China. The issue, simply put, is whether or not, first, our Armed Forces should attack military bases on the Chinese mainland; and secondly, whether or not we should use and assist Chinese Nationalist troops in an attack on the Chinese mainland. This inevitably means extending and expanding the war in Korea.

It is the policy of our Government to do everything possible to limit the present Korean war to the Korean battlefield. It is the firm determination of our Government and our allies not to extend and expand the conflict to the mainland of Asia by any action of ours. The risk involved in a further expansion of the conflict is a possibility of World War III and the full-scale intervention of the Soviet Union. It should be remembered that the Soviet Union has a treaty of alliance and assistance with the Red Chinese Government. This treaty calls for Soviet military assistance in case China is attacked by Japan or any power associated with Japan. Today we are the prime occupiers of Japan. We are associated with Japan. We are now preparing to conclude a treaty with Japan. It is entirely possible that the Soviet Union, under the obligations of her treaty with Communist China, would take direct military action were we to advance to the Chinese mainland. The political policy of the United States Government and its allies is to bring the Korean War to a conclusion and to negotiate an honorable peace. . . .

Is it not possible that the strategy of the Soviet is to trick us into a major war in Asia so that an all-out attack can be launched in Western Europe? It is Western Europe that Russia needs. It is Western Europe that has the industrial production, the skilled manpower and the strategic positions that are needed to round out the Soviet military machine. Russia and her satellites have an overabundance of population. They lack in supplies and productive machinery.

Those who support General MacArthur's position state quite confidently that the Soviet Union would not intervene were we to attack the Chinese mainland. Of course, no one really knows what the Soviet will do. But, I call to your attention that General MacArthur clearly stated to the President on the occasion of the President's conference on Wake Island in October 1950, that the Red Chinese armies would not intervene in Korea. I call this to your attention because then as now a risk was being contemplated and a military decision was being made. The military decision was that of advancing to the Yalu River in order to destroy the North Koreans. The risk involved was whether or not the Chinese Communist armies would move into the Korean war. History now tells us the answer. The Chinese armies did come into the war and momentarily the forces of the United Nations suffered tragic losses. It is reasonable to expect that an attack upon the Chinese mainland could and would provoke open Soviet intervention. The questions that we must ask ourselves then are simply these: Do we wish to take that risk? Are we prepared at this time by military strength and mobilization to meet all-out attack by the Soviet? What would be the effect upon our Armed Forces in the area of such a Soviet attack? What would be the effect of a Soviet attack in Western Europe at this time?

It is not divulging any secret when we openly recognize that we are presently weaker in terms of military strength than our adversary. This position will change within a year but today the Soviet Union and its satellites have a much larger army and air force than the United States and its allies. It appears to me that Soviet strategy is based on trapping us into a war on the Asiatic mainland only to strike in Western Europe, destroy our allies, and overrun the Western European countries. If this should happen, we would lose the only allies we have. We would lose the productive power of European industry. We would lose the critical raw materials and the strategic bases that are now under the control and possession of our allies. We would find ourselves without friends or allies and without vitally needed raw materials.

Senator Herbert Lehman[9]

There can no longer be doubt that an unbridgeable gulf has stretched between General MacArthur's view on military and political strategy and those of the Joint Chiefs of Staff and the Commander in Chief. There can be no doubt that General MacArthur sought with all his great powers as a public figure to reverse the policies of his Government. The questions before us, then are, first, whether the President acted wisely in relieving General MacArthur on the basis of the General's refusal to accede to the policies of his Government, and, secondly, whether those policies are, in fact, sound ones, designed to meet the Nation's needs and serve the national purposes.

As for the first question, the President had no alternative. No military commander has the right to try to secure, by public appeals, approval of his own policies as against the declared policies of his Government. In this way lies utter confusion and impotence. In this way lies danger to our form of government as deadly as any which we face from abroad. . . .

Let us review for a moment exactly what General MacArthur and those who share his views urge this country to do. They urge that, among other things, we bomb Manchuria and the port cities of China; that we try to establish a naval blockade of the vast coast line of China; that we enable the troops of Chiang Kai-shek in Formosa,

[9] From U.S. Senate, 82nd Cong., 1st sess., *Congressional Record*, 97, Part 3, pp. 4229–31.

with our logistic support, to attack the mainland of China across the Formosan Straits.

Mr. President, all this sounds very simple and easy. But let us look at these proposals a little more closely.

General MacArthur and others have referred bitterly to the existence of a privileged sanctuary for Chinese troops in China. But do not we have a privileged sanctuary, in Japan, just across the Korean Straits?

What if China retaliated for our bombing of China with an air attack on Japan? What if Chinese Communist troops launched an invasion of Formosa and the Ryukyu Islands and the Bonins? What then, Mr. President?

What if China asked Russia for so-called volunteer air units to bomb Alaska? What would be the end of it? And after we had bombed China's cities, what if China, as she undoubtedly would, asked Russia to come fully to her aid, under the terms of the Russo-Chinese defense assistance pact? . . .

Finally, what leads us to hope that Chiang Kai-shek's troops would be more successful in invading the mainland of China now than these troops were in holding the mainland of China 2 years ago? Might they not throw down their arms, surrender, and melt away into the hills as Chiang's troops did so insistently and so consistently during the months of the long retreat in the face of the Communist forces, from 1946 to 1949? And if they did not surrender, but chose to fight, would we permit them to be chewed up by superior forces, or would we feel impelled to send ground troops to give support to the Nationalists? . . .

Mr. President, General MacArthur, himself, says the object is to gain a complete victory in Korea. What does he mean by a complete victory? Even if it were true—which is dubious—that if we bombed Manchuria, our forces might be able to proceed up to the Yalu River and chase the Chinese out of Korea, would that be a complete victory? Would China then solemnly promise that since her troops had been driven out of Korea, they would never return? Of course, that is ridiculous. After we reached the Yalu River, if we did, could we stop? Well, if we did, we would have, at best, another stalemate. If we stopped, Chinese forces could seize the initiative and recross the Yalu River. . . .

The only possible course would be to press on until we had conquered all of China or had subdued all her armies. How many American troops would that require? A million, 2,000,000, 10,000,000? How many casualties would result and what would be the prize? What would Russia be doing while we were thus engaged, thus involved, thus wholly bogged down in a vast country of mud, jungle, desert, mountain, and ravine?

So, Mr. President, it is one thing to say that we must press forward until victory is achieved. It is quite another to follow this statement through to its logical conclusions and implications. The eventualities I have outlined promise nothing but tragic disaster for the United States and all the free world. Yet this is the inevitable course of all-out general war with China.

NEWS MAGAZINES

New Republic[10]

The uproar that has followed the removal of General MacArthur shows how necessary that removal was. The General had made himself the head of a political clique, mainly but not wholly inside the Republican Party. Only now does the public get a chance to realize how deep was his divisive effort, or how far it had gone.

MacArthur was not a mere soldier taking orders, as he has tried to picture himself. He was the head of an open conspiracy against the policy of the government he was sworn to serve. Long before his dismissal by the President, his attitude and that of his supporters had done much to deepen the split in the American Government, to confuse and weaken our relations with the United Nations, and thereby to hamper the war effort in Korea.

The forceful action of President Truman has stripped the General of the power to interfere directly in the policies of his country any longer. MacArthur must now carry on his political activity in the open without benefit of the military disguise. The common sense of the American people will doubtless reject the undemocratic philosophy of militarism for which he stands when it is nakedly presented to them. However, the clique of which MacArthur is the mouthpiece will not be easily daunted. They are dangerous men, bound together by an evil design which they will be slow to relinquish. It is an incongruous crew made up partly of those who advocate an immediate

[10] From "MacArthur's War Party," *The New Republic,* 124 (April 23, 1951): 5–6. Copyright © 1951 by Harrison-Blaine of New Jersey, Inc. Reprinted by permission of the publisher.

world war in order to prevent one, and in part of isolationists at heart who support MacArthur on the theory that if he were given his way we could in a few months retire behind our own shores and pull them up over us. His domestic support is the Tory wing of journalism and of politics—the people who scream "Communist" at everyone who disagrees with them, the enemies of Roosevelt who are still fighting his spirit six years after he went to his grave. . . .

There will be rich and unscrupulous men for MacArthur to command in his new role. It is important, therefore, to examine what would happen if the General actually got his way.

On purely military grounds, the MacArthur policy of immediate war against China would likely be disastrous.

MacArthur appears to believe that if we engaged in total war with China, Russia would not come in. Russia and China have a mutual defense pact pledging each of them to go to war if the other is attacked by any third power. It is true that Russia has broken many pledges in recent years, but it is inconceivable that she could break this one except at a cost in prestige and power she could not afford to pay.

MacArthur believes we could win a quick victory over China; Japan made the same mistake in 1937. It is straining our military resources today to hold our own in the Korean Peninsula, with masses of South Korean troops engaged and with a dozen other UN nations giving support.

MacArthur believes that Chiang's army on Formosa could successfully invade the mainland without the use of American troops. This army of a few hundred thousand men is practically without equipment of the type needed for an invasion. Remember the long years it took the United States to prepare for the Normandy invasion, even with England as a base, and with supply lines thousands of miles shorter; multiply the difficulties of the Normandy landing by 10 and you may be somewhere near the problem a Nationalist invasion presents.

The MacArthur who makes these recommendations is certainly the one who let the entire air force in the Philippines be destroyed on the ground just after Pearl Harbor, the man who divided the army in Korea last November and let it be trapped in one of the worst military reverses of our history.

In the First and Second World Wars, the United States had powerful allies who spilled their blood for us while we were making up our minds that it was our war, too. In the struggle in Korea we were able to persuade the United Nations to join us in putting down aggression; but there would be no such action if we now went to war with Communist China on MacArthur's terms. We would lose our most important ally, Great Britain. We would lose the support of the UN, and that body would be destroyed.

To repeat in words of one syllable what everyone knows except MacArthur and his followers:

The democratic world, and most of all the US, is not yet strong enough in a military sense to fight the Communist bloc on one front, to say nothing of two. We will not be prepared to withstand attack for several years longer. The one overwhelming objective in the meantime is to try to prevent Russia from attacking in Europe which, with its tremendous industrial installations, is the one great prize in the world struggle. If we can hold Europe, we have a good prospect of holding the world; if we lose, victory is against us.

It may be that Russia will strike before we are ready, no matter what we do or don't do. But if MacArthur's advice were followed, if we plunged into the quagmire of China, Stalin would almost certainly strike in Europe, and the United States would be helpless to give the democracies of the West the aid they need and have been promised.

MacArthur's abortive "peace offer" to the Chinese Communists stopped a carefully thought-out proposal of the same character that the United Nations (with the General's knowledge) was about to make. Now that he is out of the way, efforts to end the war on an honorable basis can be pursued. The aggression against South Korea which prompted the UN to take up arms has been successfully checkmated; the invaders have been driven back across the line from which the attack was launched. The war is costing the North Koreans and the Chinese Communists a terrible price. This is the moment for a fresh, determined effort to end the war on terms which will discourage future aggression and strengthen the arm of the UN.

The antagonisms that now divide the world cannot be wiped out in short order. But the desire of peoples all over the world for peace has democracies to develop, but they are nonetheless the essential ones seldom in history been so great. Patience and steadfastness of purpose for us to cultivate today. We must perfect the defenses of the free are what is called for. These qualities are among the hardest for world, always with the objective of a future in which large armament will have no place. The presence of MacArthur in the explosive Far

East was a constant danger. His removal permits the resumption of a resolute course toward peace.

Commonweal [11]

In recent months General MacArthur chose to impose his private views on his Commander in Chief by means of a message to a veterans' convention, an unauthorized message and implied challenge to the Chinese commander in Korea, and a letter to the minority leader of the House. All told, one can only judge these actions to have been the behavior pattern of a man who put himself above the laws of courtesy and country.

MacArthur's opinion on Pacific policy—which is, that Asia is the decisive battlefield to be defended against the Communists and that therefore we should extend and not limit the Korean war—is an opinion totally in opposition to American foreign policy; in holding this opinion, MacArthur was defying the judgment of the President, the State Department, the Joint Chiefs of Staff, General Eisenhower, the majority of the United Nations and the majority of the Congress. One may, if he is an admirer of the general's, believe that the general was acting in a democratic manner, in deference to the will of the majority and in the best interests of the principle we fight for, the principle of the democratic way of life. But the burden of the proof is on him. This, it seems to us, was the behavior of a man in defiance of the majority, a man with a will-to-power that was contemptuous of the prevailing reason of the majority; this, in short, was the behavior of the self-appointed genius who always thinks he knows what is best for the ignorant masses and whose actions are in the pattern of history's long chronicle of dictators.

Maybe MacArthur was right; maybe he was one of those rare and enlightened leaders destined to show mankind the way. Certainly he had reason to be restive, since he had been in a most difficult military position ever since the United Nations was forced to defend itself on the distant and disadvantageous Korean Peninsula.

But in our judgment MacArthur was disastrously wrong and we are of the opinion that the mystique of his enlightened leadership was a cult too jealously guarded by a selected group of admirers to be genuine.

[11] From "In the Public Interest," *Commonweal*, 54 (April 20, 1951): 27–28. Reprinted by permission of Commonweal Publishing Co., Inc.

U.S. News & World Report[12]

Out of the clouds of despair and frustration, out of the months of discouragement and floundering policy has come at last a symbol of hope.

It emerged last week in every city and hamlet, in every home in America. It was the simple, unrestrained American enthusiasm and admiration for and appreciation of human courage.

It came in the form of a demonstration for Douglas MacArthur—the man who fought victoriously at the head of the "Rainbow" Division on the fields of France in World War I, the man who saw the Stars and Stripes hauled down in surrender at Bataan at the start of World War II and, undaunted, led our troops back from Australia, over the mountains of New Guinea, and, by a series of hazardous amphibious landings, came in triumph to liberate the Philippines and finally to receive the Japanese surrender in Tokyo Bay.

The chapter is unparalleled in our history. The record of General MacArthur as a soldier is unmatched in the annals of our country. No man has for so long held positions of high command on active assignment in the field, with continuing responsibilities of such transcendent importance.

But it was not to him as a soldier alone that his countrymen paid him honor. His great achievements as a statesman stand out, too. Only six years ago he was marching into a conquered country at the head of victorious armies. Today those same conquered people worship him as a friend, as a statesman who, in civil as well as military affairs—applying rare tact and an *ex*traordinary administrative capacity—implanted the roots of democracy and reform and struck a blow at militarism itself.

In the East, General MacArthur stands as a symbol of American idealism, as the very embodiment of American hopes and aspirations for the free world—for an end, as he put it in his eloquent address to Congress, to colonialism and the tyrannies of the exploiting classes, a beginning of better government and higher standards of living for the common man in Asia.

But while these finer points of statesmanship will come to be recognized more fully in time and will live long in history, the American people mingled resentment and enthusiasm in their demonstration

[12] From David Lawrence, "A Salute to Courage," *U.S. News & World Report,* 30 (April 27, 1951): 76. Copyright 1951 by U.S. News & World Report, Inc. Reprinted by permission of the publisher.

last week. They had seen a great soldier dismissed from his command at the hands of a politician. The country by its applause was repudiating petty politics—the deep freezes and the mink coats, the impulsive insults to the Marine Corps and the whole sickening list of acts which are beneath the dignity and the good taste and the good manners of a President of the United States.

Yes, as Commander in Chief, he can, as in a totalitarian state, "purge" high military officers.

Yes, he can remove the head of the Navy, as he did in October 1949, for daring to testify under oath before a congressional committee and tell the truth about our naval weaknesses.

Yes, he can summarily dismiss the head of our occupation forces in Japan, where no disregard of "orders" has even been charged.

And, yes, he can with one blow impose the sentence of death on the military record of a great General and detach him from his command so quickly that he could not have that final privilege so dear to a military man—to say a few words of farewell to his troops.

Yes, he has the legal right to do all this.

But, as President Truman sought to punish General MacArthur, he forgot that ingrained in all of us is a sense of fairness which no official reprimand can tarnish or destroy.

In acclaiming Douglas MacArthur, however, the American people are primarily paying tribute to the American soldier of today—the men who die for us in Korea while an unmoral and weak-kneed Administration preaches defeatism even as it seeks, by innuendoes and smears, to persuade the American people that the whole episode is just a disobedience of "orders."

The welcome to MacArthur means that the American people are grateful for the valor and sacrifices of their sons on the field of battle. They are not cynical as the bands play and the flag flies. Like the members of Congress and veteran military officers who stood in tears in the House of Representatives last week and applauded a great man —they are not ashamed to cry.

For this still is America—the America of our forefathers, the America of the illustrious years of past history, the America that will some day see through the guilt of phony liberalism and cynical disdain for patriotism and love of fatherland.

This America that General MacArthur aroused is not an America of petty politics and tricky manipulation of public power. It is not an America of "double talk" which denounces yet embraces appeasement. It is not an America of cowardice. It is an America of resoluteness and courage and sacrifice. It is an America that applauds the man of honest convictions. It is an America that demands and must have a new leadership.

Time[18]

The drama of MacArthur's removal and homecoming obscures a far more important fact: President Truman has brought his foreign policy into the open.

This policy, new in the sense that it was publicly stated for the first time, denies to the United States the efficient use of its power, guarantees to the enemy the initiative he now has, promises that the United States will always fight on the enemy's terms. The policy invites the enemy, world communism, to involve the United States in scores of futile wars or in messy situations like Iran. Up to now world war III has been prevented by the fact that the United States is stronger than communism. The new policy almost certainly brings world war III closer because it throws away a large part of United States strength.

Truman's speech marked the reversal of a trend: Until April 11 Washington had been veering toward what might be called "the MacArthur view." Not MacArthur, but the pressure of events, was driving many civilian and military policy makers—including Truman—toward a positive, active, hopeful, constructive policy of how to combat Communist aggression. For weeks newsmen have been hearing from the mouths of some of Truman's closest advisers that the passive policy of Dean Acheson—"wait until the dust settles" in Asia—was losing out. George Marshall himself was said to be getting very interested in new countermeasures against the Chinese Communists.

But when Truman needed—or thought he needed—a defense for firing MacArthur he turned to Acheson for a brief. Acheson gave him one, prepared several days before for the purpose of defending Acheson's general viewpoint. Revised for the special situation, this speech was admirably suited to the purpose Truman had in mind—charging MacArthur with trying to extend the war. Apparently it did not occur to Truman or Acheson that the speech could have another—and far greater—effect: Giving communism world-wide possession of the strategic initiative.

[18] From "MacArthur v. Truman," *Time, The Weekly Newsmagazine*, 57 (April 23, 1951): 31–33. Copyright 1951 by Time, Inc. Reprinted by permission of the publisher.

THE PRESS [14]

New York Herald Tribune

He virtually forced his own removal. In high policy as in war there is no room for a divided command. With one of those strokes of boldness and decision which are characteristic of Mr. Truman in emergencies, a very difficult and dangerous problem has been met in the only way it could have been met.

New York Journal-American

A crushing blow to America long prepared by the clique of Administration officials who seem determined upon a course of appeasement toward Communist Russia and Communist China. It follows the line of weak-kneed diplomacy so long advocated by the Socialist Government of England, by the French and Italian Communist blocs, and by those diluted Americans who believe that the Kremlin can be diverted from its dream of world conquest by the sacrifice of its greatest and most determined opponent.

Chicago Tribune

President Truman must be impeached and convicted. His hasty and vindictive removal of Gen. MacArthur is the culmination of a series of acts which have shown that he is unfit, morally and mentally, for his high office. Mr. Truman can be impeached for usurping the power of Congress when he ordered American troops to the Korean front without a declaration of war. He can be impeached, also, for surrounding himself with grafters and incompetents. The American nation has never been in greater danger. It is led by a fool who is surrounded by knaves.

Christian Science Monitor

[The conflict over foreign policy in Asia] is embittered and confused by personal and partisan conflict. But behind these lies a question of fundamental policy. It is bigger than General MacArthur, bigger than President Truman. Unless the basic policies of the United

[14] From the *New York Times*, April 12, 1951: pp. 14–15. Copyright © 1951 by The New York Times Company. Reprinted by permission.

States and the United Nations were to be overturned, it became necessary for General MacArthur to conform, to resign, or to be removed.

DEAN ACHESON: THE GENERAL IN RETROSPECT [15]

As one looks back in calmness, it seems impossible to overestimate the damage that General MacArthur's willful insubordination and incredibly bad judgment did to the United States in the world and to the Truman Administration in the United States. During the Senate hearings a good deal of discussion revolved about whether the General had disobeyed orders in a court-martial sense of the phrase. I believe that he probably did not and that the debate is beside the point. The General was surely bright enough to understand what his Government wanted him to do. General Ridgway, who succeeded him, understood perfectly and achieved the desired ends. MacArthur disagreed with the desired ends, and wished instead to unify Korea by force of arms even though this plan would involve general war with China and, quite possibly, with the Soviet Union as well. Indeed, far from being dismayed by this prospect, he seemed, as his letter to Congressman Martin strongly suggests, to welcome the wider war, for it was in Asia, as he saw it, that "the Communist conspirators [i.e., the Soviet Union and China] have elected to make their play for global conquest, and that we [i.e., he] have joined the issue thus raised on the battlefield." Having joined the issue thus raised on the Asian battlefield, he was willing, not to say eager, to fight it out there. This was exactly what his Government had told him, beginning with the directive of September 27 and continuing until his relief, that it would not do, even if to avoid it involved withdrawal from Korea. Nevertheless he pressed his will and his luck to a shattering defeat.

In appraising its consequences, two conclusions stand out: the defeat with its losses of men and national prestige was quite avoidable had he followed the agreed plan of campaign; the defeat and MacArthur's conduct in defeat profoundly changed both the national attitude toward the war and our allies' confidence in the judgment and leadership of the United States Government and, especially, in its control over General MacArthur. Regarding the first conclusion, we have already noted that when General Ridgway took over command of the Eighth Army and later the supreme command, he was able,

[15] From Dean Acheson, *Present at the Creation* (New York: W. W. Norton & Company, Inc., 1969), pp. 526–28. Copyright © 1969 by Dean Acheson. Reprinted by permission of the publisher.

starting much farther south, after a defeat and opposed by a strong enemy, to stabilize the front as MacArthur had been told to do and to hold it. Had General MacArthur, who faced no opposition after Inchon and the defeat of the North Koreans, occupied one of the strong positions in mid-Korea, fortified it, and kept his forces collected, he could have shattered a Chinese assault just as Ridgway did.

The effect of defeat and the General's ill-concealed disaffection upon domestic and foreign confidence were equally plain. The enthusiasm with which our people and allies received President Truman's bold leadership of the United Nations in military resistance to aggression survived even the hard fighting of the retreat to the Pusan perimeter and the surprising discovery of North Korean military competence and toughness. It was heightened by the September victories and the complete collapse of the invasion of South Korea. Opinion at home and abroad would have remained steady and united had the Army under the September 27 plan and directive sealed off the South from further attack until the war should peter out, as it eventually did, even though this would require, as it also did, some hard fighting to prove the strength of the line.

What lost the confidence of our allies were MacArthur's costly defeat, his open advocacy of widening the war at what they rightly regarded as unacceptable risks, and the hesitance of the Administration in asserting firm control over him. What disturbed and divided our own people was the stream of propaganda flowing out of Tokyo that the cause of MacArthur's disasters was not his own stubborn folly, but conspiracy in Washington, probably inspired by concern for national interests other than our own. The method and source of propaganda are well illustrated by a later effusion of MacArthur's Chief of Staff, General Courtney Whitney: "Who it was who won over President Truman's confidence and corrupted his logic to the extent of defying the experienced advice of his best military experts, has always been a well-kept Washington secret. Certainly the Secretary of Defense, Louis Johnson, did not favor this kind of appeasement. So the likely person to bear the enormous blame for this incalculable mistake would seem to be the then Secretary of State Dean Acheson, possibly acting under pressure from the British Foreign Office." . . .

That General Whitney included all persons in high office in the plot against his hero is clear. . . . The continued seepage of this poison, like that administered by McCarthy, had a highly toxic effect on the American public. Like McCarthy's, it was skillfully used by the Republican right and had an effect in undermining confidence in the very institution of government in areas far wider than those where such slanderous nonsense was believed. Like air pollution, one did not have to believe in it to be poisoned by it.

This loss of confidence at home and abroad in the conduct of our foreign affairs was not the proximate cause of any change in our foreign policy, but it added to our difficulties and by so doing diminished increased energy spent on countering unwise proposals we shall see as one manifestation of this. Another was to be growing opposition in our effectiveness. The loss of support in the United Nations and the other parts of the world to the policies and interests of the United States.

23
Late Career

After the great furor of 1951, MacArthur's name gradually dropped out of the headlines, and he passed the last decade of his life in relative obscurity. Some supporters prepared campaign literature in an attempt to capture the Republican Presidential nomination for the general, but it was a small-scale and hopeless task. To large numbers of Americans, however, MacArthur remained a symbol of American military strength and traditions. Senator Thomas Dodd's address to Congress in 1961 tells much about the sources of MacArthur's continuing appeal. After his death in 1964, few critical remarks were heard; even liberal pacifists, like Roger Baldwin, found favorable aspects to his character. He had passed beyond the realm of controversy to become a national monument.

DRAFT MACARTHUR FOR PRESIDENT (1952)[1]

Draft MacArthur for President of the U.S.

Why?   14 Reasons:

1. The present crisis requires a man whose character and background are above reproach.
2. He is THE most loved, revered and respected living American.
3. He has been greeted and cheered and praised by more human beings than any individual in the history of the world.
4. Every evil force on earth hates General Douglas MacArthur. He has made the right enemies.
5. A confidential poll of the 1948 delegates to the Republican Convention reveals that MacArthur is their overwhelming favorite.
6. The Truman bureaucracy fears MacArthur as no other potential candidate. His youthful mind, his strong body, plus his rich experience qualify him above all other public figures.
7. He is a Christian statesman in the truest sense of the word.
8. He stands head and shoulders above any man in either party now being considered for the Presidency.
9. Any announced candidate should consider it as great an honor to be Vice President with MacArthur as to be President without him.
10. He has radio appeal, television appeal and radiates a dynamic masculine personality after the order of George Washington.

[1] From Draft MacArthur Committee, "Draft MacArthur for President of the U.S.," Campaign Literature (1952), Vassar College Library.

11. His willingness to risk his entire career rather than to obey the compromising pygmies of Washington demonstrates that he loves America more than honors, military prestige or position.

12. His character, self-respect and statesmanship rise above the babblings of partisanism. His great mind and soul are cast on the side of righteousness and pitted against the forces of unrighteousness. He loves America—he hates Communism. He is completely devoted to patriotism in its truest sense. He hates treason, appeasement and defeatism.

13. The devotion of his personal staff and the warm radiation of his family circle mark him as one who enjoys the deep and genuine respect of those who are the most intimately associated with him.

14. He can win a victory which will cross geographical lines which will recognize no class barriers, and when it is won it will be a victory so convincing and so clean and so dynamic that every true American will know that the redemption of our nation is at hand.

SENATOR THOMAS J. DODD: THE MEANING OF MACARTHUR (1961) [2]

. . . Tomorrow Gen. Douglas MacArthur will return to the United States after once more successfully completing an important mission for our country.

His trip to the Philippines has been called a sentimental journey; and it has been that, not only for him and the people of the Philippines, but for all of us.

The sight of General MacArthur in uniform, as of old, receiving the plaudits of admiring millions, recalls vividly to our minds the picture of our Nation as we would always hope to see it, a nation that had kept its promise, a nation victorious on all fronts, a nation at the pinnacle of worldly power and esteem, a nation triumphantly dedicated to the cause of freedom.

To millions of people at home and around the globe, Douglas MacArthur has seemed a symbol and almost a personification of America in its finest aspects.

Outwardly there was the unforgettable surface picture, the striking countenance, the confident stride, the legendary hat and glasses and corncob pipe, the resonant, authoritative voice, the grand phrase, the dramatic gesture; and behind this surface picture were all the attributes of excellence, the supreme competence, the serene confidence,

[2] From U.S. Senate, 87th Cong., 1st sess., *Congressional Record,* 107, Part 9, pp. 12380–81.

the intellectual power, the noble purpose, the complete commitment to the vision of an America that was unconquerable in the service of a just cause.

General MacArthur must always have felt in his bones that electric current of excitement which America and things American brought to the world two centuries ago; and he has had the rare capacity to radiate that current to the people of his time.

Here is a man with a sense of history, with a flair for what is honestly and genuinely dramatic, with an ability to surround himself with an aura of romance and mystery, all effectively and wisely used to advance our national interest.

The name of Douglas MacArthur causes to flash through the mind unforgettable images which are an essential part of the American story: The gallant, magnificent defense of Bataan and Corregidor against hopeless odds; the promise to return and the depth of conviction that made men believe the promise would be kept; the vast, brilliant, island-hopping campaign stretching from Australia to Tokyo which will ever remain a marvel of military genius; the wading ashore at Leyte; the incomparable scene on the battleship *Missouri* where General MacArthur accepted the surrender of our enemy, appropriately concluding a victory so awesome, so complete, so seemingly final; and then the restoration of that fallen enemy, to freedom, social justice, and prosperity.

But if the name of Douglas MacArthur recalls to each of us the supreme hour of national triumph, so too it compels us to face up to the tragic and anguishing picture of our national retreat from that triumph. If General MacArthur was the most eminent spokesman of the American tradition of victory, so also was he the preeminent and perhaps the pivotal casualty of our departure from that tradition.

He had told us:

In war there is no substitute for victory.

And that statement was not only an expression of military certainty, but an affirmation of the indomitable spirit which this Nation had historically displayed.

The Korean war and the events surrounding it ruptured that tradition. It ushered something new into American policy.

From then on, fear, indecision, vacillation, the counsels of defeat, of weakness, of appeasement gained a beachhead that has since spread and grown.

The controversy which resulted in the dismissal of General Mac-

Arthur and the ensuing loss of the Korean war may prove to have been the turning point in American history, for it marked the first conscious decision by this Nation to accept defeat rather than run the necessary risks of victory.

If the cause of those who support an unyielding policy against Communist aggression could not prevail then, we may well ask ourselves: When can it prevail?

For then, all of the elements were favorable to it.

The United States alone possessed significant nuclear power.

We were engaged in active, open warfare against the Communist criminals and, therefore, our leaders and our people had every reason to be fully aware of the nature of the enemy.

Tens of thousands of our sons were casualties in a war which was being fought aimlessly with one hand tied behind their back.

There was a wave of national protest and disgust at our failure to push the Korean fighting to the victorious conclusion that was within our grasp.

And in General MacArthur, those who stood for victory had as their champion, not only one of the most revered and respected figures of American history, but also one of the most articulate spokesmen that any cause has ever had.

Who can forget the outpouring of sentiment for MacArthur and the cause he represented that swept this country from end to end when he returned to the United States in the spring of 1951?

I have always been convinced that the overwhelming majority of the American people supported the policies which he then outlined as a means of winning the Korean war.

Yet somehow this sentiment failed to translate itself into effective political action.

In the election campaign of 1952, neither party advocated a policy of victory in Korea.

The Democrats stood pat with the policies that led to the sad ouster of General MacArthur.

The Republicans seemed mainly interested, not in winning the Korean war, but in blaming the Democrats for it and in extricating the United States from it.

And so, in a decision for which we as a nation can truly be held responsible, the opportunity to crush the aggressive power of Communist China at its outset was lost by default and America proceeded upon a policy of vacillation and retreat from victory which, with each passing year, brings its harvest of shame and defeat.

For almost a decade General MacArthur has remained aloof from the storm center of political controversy.

His return to the scene of his greatest hours has deeply stirred this Nation and the world.

The universal acclaim for General MacArthur which has swept through the Philippines is in my mind more than just a deserved tribute to a very great hero.

It is as well the symptom of a yearning there and throughout the world for that dynamic, resolute, indomitable American leadership of which General MacArthur was and is the symbol.

There was a time in history when a nation could live for a century and more on the achievements and the example of a man such as Douglas MacArthur.

That time has passed.

But it can be truly said that in this century, in peace and in war, when the vital interests of our country have been placed in the hands of this great man, they have been preserved and advanced.

Tomorrow the soldier will be home once more.

The esteem and love and thanks of a grateful nation go out to him for what he has done, for what he is, and for what he means to our generation and to all generations.

ROGER BALDWIN (1964)[3]

Since I knew General MacArthur for only a brief three months while he was Supreme Commander in Japan, it may seem presumptuous of me to comment on him. I do so only because I bear witness to a side of the General that is little appreciated; it was opened to me in an unexpectedly understanding relationship.

On his invitation, I had come to Japan as a private citizen to assist the Japanese in protecting their new civil liberties. Challenged to transform a feudal, militaristic nation into a peaceful democracy, General MacArthur had embarked on what he called a crusade. I found at once in him qualities that a great military career had concealed—a profound commitment to democratic liberties, an instinct for the equality of peoples, a respect for the sensitivities of the defeated Japanese and a reformer's zeal.

Relations with the Japanese were so skillfully handled that they led into a veritable revolution. Popular forces were released for complete

[3] From Roger Baldwin, "General Douglas MacArthur," *Nation*, 198 (April 20, 1964): 385. Reprinted by permission of the publisher.

political freedom, for a democratic economic order with full trade-union liberties and a vast distribution of land to farmers, and for the emancipation of women. These among many other reforms shook up Japanese institutions from the Emperor to the police.

I witnessed the first test of the new order, under the new constitution renouncing militarism and establishing democracy, when the first election brought to office a Christian Socialist Prime Minister. This election won the General's warm approval, and the spirit that welcomed the results of a free election accepted the principles of civil liberties without question. Not once did I have reason to differ with the General. It is largely to his credit that Japan today has the most effective system for protecting citizens' rights of any nation outside the West.

General MacArthur took profound pride in the renunciation of war in the new Japanese constitution, remarking to me that it was a "shining example which all nations eventually must follow." Stanchly internationalist, he favored a peace treaty long before it came, with a Japan ready, he said, to join the United Nations: "The Japanese," he added, "have already joined it in their hearts."

On the personal side of General MacArthur, as revealed in my conferences, I found nothing to bear out the often-cited impression of vain egotism. He was ever responsive and considerate, as eager to listen as to talk. I heard from many that his appearance of vanity in public was in reality a mask for self-consciousness. He was eloquent even in private conversation, but a very easy man to converse with. His rhetorical public prose struck me as just a studied elaboration of his natural eloquence.

I am aware that General MacArthur impressed people quite differently, and doubtless he was a contradictory character. A friendly fellow-general once remarked to me that he had about him a bit of Dr. Jekyll and Mr. Hyde. That may help explain his appeal to both reactionaries and liberals. But however one judges his historic role, none would deny the impressive impact he made on all by powerful human qualities: his deep dedication to whatever he undertook, his sense of justice, his high principles and his firm ideals. It was a privilege to witness their expression in the memorable days of his one historic civilian role. It was the role in which, as a man of peace, he said he hoped most to be remembered.

PART THREE

DOUGLAS MACARTHUR IN HISTORY

> *No completed scholarly biography of MacArthur yet
> exists; however, specific aspects and chronological periods of his
> career have recently been investigated by historians and political
> scientists. In general, scholars have not dealt as kindly with
> MacArthur as have many of his more popular biographers, in-
> cluding the often adulatory former members of his staff. In the
> years before his death, the general observed with some pique:
> "The historans are jumping on me."*

24
D. Clayton James[1]

> *The recent first volume of D. Clayton James' projected
> two-volume biography of MacArthur is perhaps the most pains-
> taking scholarly account thus far of the general's life. Although
> seeking, usually successfully, to avoid the extremes of damnation
> or adulation so characteristic of books about MacArthur, James
> exhibits a pro-military bias which often leads him to a favorable
> assessment of the general's career. In this selection, he discusses
> MacArthur's work as superintendent of West Point. Two aspects
> of the West Point experience are harbingers of MacArthur's later
> career: his curious emergence as a reformer (as in Japan), and
> his bitter personal relations with the Pershing "faction" of the
> Army (as with George C. Marshall).*

. . . When he reported to Chief of Staff March, MacArthur
was promptly told that he was to assume the superintendency at West
Point. . . .

. . . "West Point is forty years behind the times," March stated
bluntly. . . . The chief of staff's instructions to MacArthur were suc-
cinct: "Revitalize and revamp the Academy." . . .

---

[1] From D. Clayton James, *The Years of MacArthur: 1880–1941* (Boston: Hough-
ton Mifflin Company, 1970), vol. 1, pp. 261, 263–65, 267, 270–72, 274, 278–79, 287–
89, 292–94. Copyright © 1970 by D. Clayton James. Reprinted by permission of
the publisher.

Despite his initial protest over the assignment, MacArthur really welcomed the opportunity to take the reins at West Point. Although most of its almuni felt a strong attachment to the school, MacArthur's loyalty and affection for his alma mater were unusually deep and seemed to grow with the years. Besides, the superintendency was one of the most prestigious jobs in the Army. MacArthur's holding of the position was probably a paramount factor in his promotion to the permanent rank of brigadier general in January, 1920, when most regular officers and brevet generalships had already been reduced to their permanent ranks of prewar days. This enabled him to pull well ahead of other officers of his age and experience, most of whom did not attain brigadier general again until the Second World War. But foremost in MacArthur's mind at the time was a burning desire to reform West Point. . . .

. . . In molding the new kind of military leader at West Point, MacArthur aimed "to introduce a new atmosphere of liberalization in doing away with provincialism, a substitute of subjective for objective discipline, a progressive increase of cadet responsibility . . . to broaden the curriculum so as to be abreast of the best modern thought on education, to bring West Point into a new and closer relationship with the Army at large."

. . . The professors felt that they were the ones most responsible for preserving the hallowed traditions and standards of the institution. They were not favorably impressed by a reform-minded superintendent who wanted to turn the system upside down and then depart in a few years, leaving them with the shambles. Most important, the professors had the voting power to prevent significant changes to which they were opposed. . . .

An early and lasting dispute developed when MacArthur told the members of the academic board that more stress must be placed on the social sciences. In line with his aim to produce officers who understood human motivations and were knowledgeable about national and foreign affairs, he urged the introduction of courses in political science, economics, sociology, and psychology; enlargement of the offerings in English and history; and the creation of a department of economics, government, and history. . . . The academic board grudgingly gave MacArthur a few tidbits, but nothing more. . . .

MacArthur did not attempt to inaugurate an elective system, but he did make a sound start toward broadening and modernizing the curriculum. Entrance requirements were considerably stiffened. Moreover, new instructors were required to spend the first year of their appointment studying at civilian universities in the disciplines they would teach at the academy. Also, extensive changes were made in the tactical department to update the cadets' education in supply, procurement, and modern ordnance. . . .

MacArthur was never satisfied with the daily recitation method of education, which was used by all of the departments. Most colleges had long abandoned the recitation as an ineffective instructional method. In his first year MacArthur announced that the "front-board recitation" was not to be considered as mandatory "in subjects which do not lend themselves readily to it." Hoping to get the cadets out of "the habit of just going along by rote," he encouraged instructors to allow less time for routine reciting and more time for lectures, class discussions, laboratory work in the physical sciences, and oral drills in foreign languages. . . .

. . . The old guard's loudest outcries were heard when MacArthur began to relax discipline and allow privileges to the cadets which were unthinkable in West Point's previous history. . . . MacArthur shocked the traditionalists by allowing first classmen to take six-hour weekend leaves off the reservation, set up a first classmen's club in Church Hall, and enjoy limited fraternization with post officers. . . . The three upper classes were allowed to elect class officers for the first time, and upperclassmen were permitted to start a cadet newspaper. . . .

With the advent of the Harding administration in the spring of 1921, John W. Weeks, a wealthy Boston broker and not an acquaintance of MacArthur, took over as Secretary of War. More significant, a few months later a general was appointed chief of staff whom MacArthur knew only too well: Pershing. Like March, Pershing had served under MacArthur's father, but . . . misunderstandings and sharp exchanges had occasionally marred the relations between Pershing and MacArthur on the fields of France. . . .

. . . While reminding the executive and legislative branches of the federal government that "our present combat strength will be insufficient to fulfill the functions required by our national defense policy," he and the War Department meekly accepted the separation of civilian and military powers and their subordination to civilian controls. . . . MacArthur's outspokennesss in endeavoring to secure more funds for West Point must have irritated Weeks and Pershing. Also, the intense pace of the superintendent's reforms at West Point, as well as the nature of those changes, must have been contrary to their wishes. . . .

Suddenly, on November 22, 1921, Pershing notified MacArthur: "It is important, I think, that you be made aware of the decision of the War Department to make the regulation with reference to foreign service applicable to the entire officer personnel of the Army. The roster shows you to be high up for this service. . . ." He continued: "I am writing now to advise you that at the end of the present school year you will be available for a tour of service beyond the limits of the United States." . . . MacArthur was surprised, apparently thinking that he would be allowed a four-year term as superintendent. . . .

At the end of January, 1922, Pershing announced the appointment of Brigadier General Fred W. Sladen, commanding officer at Fort Sheridan, Illinois, as MacArthur's successor at the end of the academic year. . . . He had established a creditable record in the A.E.F., but he was known to be a staunch conservative on Army policies. . . .

. . . MacArthur's place on the foreign-duty list served as a convenient pretext for removing a refractory individualist who created difficulties and embarrassments for the War Department in its relations with Congress, the White House, and the conservative alumni of West Point. . . . The War Department in the early 1920's was enjoying a season of reaction, and had no room in the higher echelons of the military establishment for a liberal reformer. . . . MacArthur was ousted by traditionalism. . . .

. . . Many aspects of MacArthur's long career are still controversial, but in the Long Gray Line there is general agreement that he, more than any other man, led West Point across the threshold into the rapidly changing world of modern military education. Indeed, his pioneering efforts at the United States Military Academy rank as one of his most important contributions to the development of the modern Army.

25

William E. Leuchtenburg[1]

> *In this selection from his historical study of Depression era politics, William E. Leuchtenburg places the onus for the decision to rout the Bonus Army upon President Herbert Hoover. He implies, however, that MacArthur bore the responsibility for the severity with which he implemented that decision.*

Through the month of June, 1932, singing the old war songs and bearing placards "Cheered in '17, Jeered in '32," veterans of World War I massed on Washington to petition Congress to pay them at once war service bonuses Congress had agreed to pay in 1945. They set up a large shanty town on the Anacostia Flats outside the capital, and when they overran the flats, they took over some land and unused government buildings on Pennsylvania Avenue. At its height, the Bonus Army numbered over twenty thousand. When Congress rejected this petition in boots reminiscent of Coxey's march of forty years before, some of the veterans went home, but many others, homeless, jobless, and aimless, stayed on in Washington.

The encampment of the Bonus Army presented the head of the District police, Pelham Glassford, who had been the youngest brigadier general in the A.E.F., with a difficult problem. He opposed the bonus and had tried to discourage the men from coming; when they refused to leave, he tried to lure them home by having the Marine Band play "Carry Me Back to Old Virginny" and "My Old Kentucky Home." Yet he reasoned that, although the men were encamped illegally, their only offense was poverty. If they could have afforded it, they would have booked rooms in downtown hotels like other petitioners. His motorcycle cops furnished iodine and pills to the veterans, played baseball with them, gave them advice on digging latrines, even furnished some tents and bedding. For a time General Glassford handled the finances of the Bonus Army. He believed the greatest mistake the government could make would be a show of violence.

Glassford's composure was not matched by that of Hoover and his

[1] From William E. Leuchtenburg, *Franklin D. Roosevelt and the New Deal, 1932–1940* (New York: Harper & Row, Publishers, 1963), pp. 13–16. Copyright © 1963 by William E. Leuchtenburg. Reprinted by permission of the publisher.

aides. As the Bonus Army squatted down for what might be a protracted stay, Hoover lost his sense of proportion and some of his more volatile lieutenants panicked. The White House was put under guard, the gates chained, the streets about it cleared of people—all of which added to the impression that the President had cut himself off from the country. Then, precipitately, the administration decided it must have immediate possession of the unused buildings which the veterans had occupied. On July 28, Glassford reluctantly undertook the assignment of dislodging the veterans. Two brief skirmishes ensued, in one of which two veterans were killed. The Commissioners now had the pretext for requesting federal troops, and Hoover and Secretary of War Patrick Hurley, who was convinced he faced a Communist uprising of menacing proportions, quickly obliged. The Army, under General Douglas MacArthur, carried out its mission with few casualties, but with a thoroughness that the situation scarcely required. Four troops of cavalry with drawn sabers, six tanks, and a column of steel-helmeted infantry with fixed bayonets entered downtown Washington. After clearing the buildings on Pennsylvania Avenue, they crossed the Anacostia Bridge, thousands of veterans and their wives and children fleeing before them, routed the bonusers from their crude homes, hurled tear gas bombs into the colony, and set the shacks afire with their torches. That night, Washington was lit by the burning camps of Anacostia Flats.

Hoover's use of armed force against American veterans raised a storm of protest. "What a pitiful spectacle is that of the great American Government, mightiest in the world, chasing unarmed men, women and children with army tanks," observed the Washington *News*. The administration made matters still worse by vilifying the Bonus Army as a rabble of Communists and criminals. General MacArthur described the marchers as "a mob . . . animated by the essence of revolution." If the President had let the "insurrectionists" carry on for one more week, MacArthur stated, "the institutions of our Government would have been very severely threatened." Far from being a menacing band of revolutionaries, the Bonus Army was a whipped, melancholy group of men trying to hold themselves together when their spirit was gone. The Communist faction had to be protected from other bonus marchers who threatened physical violence. There were some criminals in the group, but as one commentator remarked, the record for serious crime in President Harding's cabinet was proportionately higher than in the B.E.F. Washington experienced more crime in August after the Army had departed than in July when it was there. To cap the episode, the administration claimed the U.S. Army had been guilty of no violence, and had not fired the camp, two statements which the newsreels belied.

26
Richard Rovere and
Arthur Schlesinger, Jr.[1]

Journalist Richard Rovere and historian Arthur Schlesinger, Jr. teamed up, in 1951, to produce a biting critique of the general and his views on United States foreign policy. Although the book opened many formerly unknown aspects of MacArthur's career to public scrutiny, it was rather obviously a work of political partisanship, motivated by their desire to defend the beleaguered Truman Administration in its hour of need.

. . . MacArthur is a man of advanced years—he turned seventy-one three months before his recall—but he is vigorous, and there are no known limits to his ambitions. In 1944 and 1948, he was a figure to be reckoned with in Republican presidential politics. He did not himself endorse the MacArthur candidacy, but he did not—except very late in the preconvention campaign—discourage the MacArthur booms. As he himself put it, "I can say with due humility that I would be recreant to all my concepts of good citizenship were I to shrink because of the hazards and responsibilities involved from accepting any public duty to which I might be called by the American people." Barkis was willing; whether he is now eager is impossible to say. But there are portents. In the delirium that surrounded his speech to Congress, it passed almost without comment that, later in the same afternoon, he made a brief, patriotic address to the convention of the Daughters of the American Revolution. "The complexities and confusion," he told the transported ladies of illustrious descent, "resulting largely from internal subversion and corruption and detailed regimentation over our daily lives now threaten the country no less than it was threatened in Washington's day. Under these harmful influences, we have drifted far away . . . from the simple but immutable pattern etched by our forefathers." In subsequent speeches to state legislatures, he would enlarge upon this theme.

This country has not seen many personalities like MacArthur's. It

is striking that the man who has shown himself to have so overpowering an appeal to millions of Americans, an appeal that is largely in-
dependent of doctrine and is capable of inducing a kind of mass
amnesia in the susceptible, is not cast in any of the typical American
molds. This is not to say that there is anything un-American or sinis-
tral about him but merely that the elements of his style cannot easily be
associated with those traits which Americans possess, or hope to possess,
themselves and which in normal circumstances they respond to with
warmth. He is lofty and impersonal. Though he has little self-concern,
he has great manifest self-regard. He prides himself on his austerity.
Once, reading a manuscript of an article about himself, he penciled
in a suggestion that he be characterized as "austere" rather than, as
the author had it, "remote." Of course, he is remote, too, as any man
must be when he is the object of a passionate and competitive adoration in his entourage, and when he has an overriding sense of mission
and destiny. He is commanding, imperious, imperial, ascetic, humor-
less, flamboyant, not necessarily pompous but full of pomp.

As a military man, MacArthur's punctilio separates him by light
years from generals like Omar Bradley and Dwight Eisenhower, who
represent a type which up to now has had great appeal to a people
retaining ancestral memories of a day when the militia elected its own
officers. If he is close to anything, it is to the French military tradition
—St. Cyr and the Polytechnique—and to the Bismarckian tradition
in statesmanship. He knew "the trade of being a king," a knowledge
which has served him and his country well in Japan, without ever
being taught it.

As illustration, take a simple contrast between MacArthur and Eisenhower.

Eisenhower had a well-publicized habit, in the last war, of greeting
some previously unknown enlisted man by extending a hand and
saying, "My name's Eisenhower." In a sense, the act may have been
disingenuous. It had been suggested to him by a celebrated war cor-
respondent, who explained that it would make a nice front-page box
for newspapers throughout the world, which it certainly did. It was a
fake, but the point is that it was a particular kind of fake. Eisenhower's ready acceptance of the idea showed not only that he was, in
fine American style, game for a good publicity stunt, but that he was
prepared, at a time when the world was ready to compare him to
Caesar and Hannibal and Alexander, to have the world think of him
as a blood brother to the traveling salesman. MacArthur's approach
was different. When he strode ashore at Leyte, his little speech, no

doubt as well-rehearsed as Eisenhower's, was "I have returned. Rally to me. Let no heart be faint."

MacArthur's Caesaresque words may very well have been better suited to the occasion than Eisenhower's. After all, it was important to give people a sense of confidence, to ask them to take up the American cause, and it was not at all important, not immediately important anyway, to have people look upon their liberator as an unspoiled son of Abilene. But Eisenhower's words were those of a man who adhered to an American tradition, while MacArthur's were those of a man who seemed to be deliberately rejecting the tradition of Grant and Joe Hooker and the McAuliffe who simply said "Nuts" at Bastogne and, in particular, of the Commodore Schley, who, after the Battle of Santiago, said "There is glory enough for all."

The sources of personal power are too deep for definition—except by great artists and, sometimes, by psychoanalysts. How one man thinks of himself is something no other man can say. MacArthur may or may not think of himself as a messiah, but he does have a messianic style. There was an odd episode in New York one day not long after the speech to Congress. At a conference in the Waldorf, his aide, Major General Courtney Whitney, was asked by some reporters if there was any possibility that the General might be dissimulating just a trifle when he disclaimed political aspirations. General Whitney, who always saw the press for MacArthur, said that the General had anticipated just such a question and had directed that those who asked it be referred to John 20:20–29. There, as the reporters learned after some rummaging around for a benefaction of the Gideon Society, is to be found the story of Doubting Thomas, the gloomiest apostle and the one who could not believe in the Resurrection "except that I shall see in His hands the print of the nails and thrust my hand into his side." Then Jesus appeared, and Thomas reached forth his hand, and was convinced. Jesus said, "Thomas, because thou hast seen me, thou hast believed: blessed are they that have not seen and yet have believed." It was a strange identification. . . .

Douglas MacArthur was never less than promising. He led the class of 1903 at West Point, making, it is said, the highest scholastic record anyone has ever made there. He was rousingly handsome—the late Hugh Johnson, a classmate, said young MacArthur was the best-looking man he had ever seen—and his career, both social and military, was adroitly managed by his mother, a Virginian who set great store by adroit social management. When she learned that the mother of Ulysses S. Grant III had moved to West Point to attend to her son's interests, she determined that a MacArthur should lack no advantages possessed by a Grant, so she swept up the Hudson in full sail and anchored fast for four years. It is said that she gave a superb performance.

After graduating, MacArthur served briefly in the Philippines, seeing his first action in skirmishes with brigands; was a military aide to Theodore Roosevelt; went out to Japan for a short hitch; helped seize Vera Cruz in 1914; was briefly superintendent of the old State, War, and Navy Building; and became the first press officer in War Department history. The work he turned in was always first-class. General Robert Eichelberger's first memory of MacArthur goes back to 1911 or 1912. A fairly raw second lieutenant, Eichelberger had just arrived at camp. He was told that the two coming men of the Army were there. One was Captain MacArthur; the other was Lieutenant George Catlett Marshall.

In France, MacArthur served with distinction and valor. A major by then, he proposed over the heads of his superior officers the project of a "Rainbow Division"—a kind of All-American division made up of National Guard units from many states—and when the outfit was set up, he eventually became its commander. He took part in the Champagne-Marne and Aisne-Marne defensives and in the St. Mihiel, Essey, Pannes, Meuse-Argonne and Sedan offensives. In the authoritative view of Newton D. Baker, Wilson's Secretary of War, he was the best front-line officer the country had. He was the youngest division commander in France and the youngest officer of general rank in the Army, at that time. Later, he was to be the youngest Chief of Staff and the youngest superintendent of West Point in history. The papers had found him a fetching figure and liked to call him "the D'Artagnan of the A.E.F." After serving for a while with the occupation forces in Germany, he came home with two battle wounds, a trunkful of decorations and clippings, and enough memories of adventure and wartime kudos to nourish a vast discontent through the years of peace.

In the twenties, MacArthur, like Winston Churchill and Charles de Gaulle and other figures of a heroic cast, was miserably out of place. It was no age for heroes; for a professional soldier of MacArthur's stripe, it all but was impossible. Given his limitations along with his abilities, there seemed almost nothing for him to do except do nothing. He could not fly the ocean like Lindbergh, or explore the poles like Byrd; he would not turn to business like Hugh Johnson, or to politics, like Leonard Wood. The Army was his dedication; he could conceive no alternative. Nevertheless, the United States was a wasteland, the Army a withered vine.

Luckily, he managed, after finishing up as Superintendent of West Point, which was largely a matter of distasteful bickering with Congress over money, to escape into the Philippines for a few years. This was shortly after his marriage to Louise Cromwell Brooks, a bright and giddy and very rich divorcee who provided MacArthur's one fleeting contact with the jazz age ("Marriage of Mars to Millions"—newspaper headline). Mrs. Brooks, who was the stepdaughter of Edward T. Stotesbury and who, after divorcing MacArthur married the actor Lionel Atwill, had been General Pershing's official hostess, and it was gossiped around Washington that the Manila job was an exile. Exile or not, it was, for a time, a happy return to the family fief. But even in Manila, he tasted gall. The marriage was a failure and a rather public one at that. The Manila papers were full of stories. She divorced him in Reno in 1929. He was back in Manila at the time. Late in 1935, once again in Manila, he met Jean Faircloth of Murfreesboro, Tennessee; he married her in 1937. It has been, by all accounts, a most successful marriage. In 1938, the second Mrs. MacArthur gave birth to the General's only child, Arthur. The dynasty can continue.

In spite of the two Philippine assignments, he spent most of the twenties in the United States. Those years were notable chiefly for his service on the court-martial of Brigadier General Billy Mitchell, the prophet of airpower, and for his service as President of the American Committee for the Olympic Games. The Mitchell affair is one from which he has not yet quite extricated himself. He and Mitchell had known each other as boys in Milwaukee, where the Mitchells and the MacArthurs were the most prominent military families. It seems a peculiar piece of jurisprudence to have appointed MacArthur to the court-martial, but peculiar or not, it was done. His role in the trial is still enigmatic. Certain of MacArthur's friends have claimed for years that MacArthur voted against conviction. The Luce publications assert this as a fact, and a fact it may be, but MacArthur himself, perhaps respecting the sanctity of court-martial proceedings, has never publicly disclosed his vote. . . .

Mitchell's recollection of the trial in a manuscript written in 1935 and left in the hands of friends shortly before his death in 1936 expresses not gratitude but deep resentment. Mitchell wrote:

Douglas MacArthur, I believe, will be the first to admit that I was right, when the next war comes. He regrets the part he played in my court-martial. May he be brave enough to say it openly.

27
Forrest C. Pogue[1]

During World War II, MacArthur competed for authority and resources with other theatre commanders and with rival military services. In this selection from his multi-volume biography of General George C. Marshall, the military historian Forrest Pogue describes the difficulties MacArthur's demands caused his anxious Chief of Staff.

Complicating the situation further was the presence in Australia of a senior United States Army commander whose strategic views and wounded pride made him intent on personally conducting prompt offensive action against the Japanese. His determined efforts to advance the special claims of his Southwest Pacific Theater brought him into conflict with the designs of the Navy, forcing Marshall to become deeply involved in interservice quarrels and special problems. Thus, while committed to pressing offensive operations in northwest Europe, for which he was charged with special responsibilities by the Joint Chiefs of Staff, he had to serve as a buffer between the Army and Navy leaders in the Pacific, helping to provide a measure of unity that would otherwise have been lacking. On many issues Marshall found it simpler to achieve harmony with Admiral King than with his own subordinate, General MacArthur.

A man of profound belief in his own destiny and in the rightness of his own judgments, MacArthur was convinced that the war must be won in the Pacific, that it should follow strategic concepts that he had outlined while still in the Philippines, and that it should be conducted along lines that would make his theater the center of operations. This attitude not only ignored the broad decisions taken by the Combined Chiefs of Staff but overlooked the central role of the Navy in any operation planned for the Pacific.

Political opponents of the administration created problems by proposing that MacArthur be given his head, and friends of the President made difficulties by suggesting that the Southwest Pacific commander be selected as generalissimo of the Armed Forces of the United States.

[1] From Forrest C. Pogue, *George C. Marshall: Ordeal and Hope, 1932–1942* (New York: The Viking Press, Inc., 1966), pp. 373–75. Copyright © 1966 by George C. Marshall Research Foundation. Reprinted by permission of the publisher.

The latter prospect appealed neither to Roosevelt nor to Marshall. It is not clear how soon Roosevelt feared that his critics were grooming the Pacific leader as a possible McClellan for the election of 1944, but there is evidence that as early as February 1942 at least one powerful Republican senator, Arthur Vandenberg, was thinking of MacArthur as a candidate in the next presidential election. In these circumstances MacArthur's allusions to the demands of American public opinion for certain operations he wanted to launch assumed political overtones that he probably did not intend.

In no other theater of war did Marshall have the constant hint of challenge to War Department policy that he sensed in messages from the Southwest Pacific. That no angry showdown came in the course of the war was due largely to his own forbearance and the conviction that MacArthur was especially fitted for the Pacific Command. Unfortunately his attitude was misunderstood; some of MacArthur's staff apparently concluded that Marshall was afraid to go to the mat with his former superior.

In talking after the war about operations in the Pacific, General Marshall emphasized repeatedly MacArthur's excellence as a commander and the fact that he often had to fight with almost nothing. But there were points on which the two men strongly disagreed. In speaking of his relationship with MacArthur, something he rarely did, Marshall said:

> He was of a very independent nature and he made himself a political factor from the start. . . . And the President was very careful in handling him because of that. . . . Over there [in Australia], he made beautiful use of what he got, but he spent so much time scrapping with the Navy. Halsey tried his best to please MacArthur. He tried to cooperate all the way through. MacArthur was a very fine commander. He was . . . supersensitive about everything. He thought everybody had ulterior motives about everything. . . . He was conspicuous in the matter of temperament. With Chennault in China and MacArthur in the Southwest Pacific, I sure had a combination of temperament.

Because of the potential clashes between services and personalities in the Pacific, General Marshall retained a special interest in the command organization in that area. He took the lead in securing MacArthur's appointment as the Southwest Pacific commander, winning British agreement to an arrangement whereby he exercised supreme command under the Combined Chiefs of Staff. In addition, the governments of Australia, New Zealand, and the Dutch Government-in-Exile granted MacArthur authority over their troops in the Pacific. Allied Land Forces were commanded by General Sir Thomas Blamey of Australia, Allied Naval Forces were under Vice Admiral Herbert F. Leary of the United States Navy, and Allied Air Forces were under General Brett. General Marshall twice indicated that MacArthur should emphasize the international nature of his headquarters by adding key Australian, New Zealand, and Dutch officers to his staff, but the suggestion was rather pointedly ignored.

Had it been feasible, General Marshall would have liked to unite all American forces in the Pacific under one commander, an idea to which he returned as late as 1943. His stubborn fight had won Churchill's acceptance of the concept of unified command, but he was less successful when it came to bringing MacArthur and the Navy under the same arrangement. Here he was blocked by the fact that MacArthur was quite senior to Admiral Chester W. Nimitz, the ranking naval commander in the Pacific, and could not easily serve under him, and by the Navy's flat refusal to put its carriers under the Southwest Pacific commander.

28

Edwin O. Reischauer[1]

In 1950, Edwin O. Reischauer discussed MacArthur's role in the first part of the Japanese Occupation in his history of United States relations with Japan. The distinguished Harvard scholar, who later became United States Ambassador to Japan, praised MacArthur for the excellence of his efforts, and contended that they won him the admiration of the Japanese people.

The Japanese people may have largely determined the atmosphere of the occupation, but it has been the American authorities who have guided the course of postwar Japan. Although they numbered only a few thousand individuals, backed at first by a sizable army of occupation troops but later by no more than a token force of 100,000 men or less, they have dominated the scene, making themselves an indelible part of Japanese history in one of its most crucial phases. A mere handful of men, they have vigorously and confidently undertaken the task of remaking a nation of eighty million people. The nineteen million Japanese school children and students alone roughly equal the total population of the United States zone of Germany. Except in sprawling India and China, nowhere else has so large a national group ever come under the rule of a single foreign conqueror. Never before has such a small group of men set out to work such fundamental changes in so large a mass of people. The undertaking has been gigantic. But the doughty members of the occupation approached their tasks with an enthusiasm and a firmness of purpose which made it seem almost easy.

The tone of the American occupation has been set by General MacArthur, who, by his firm domination of his own occupation personnel and the entire Japanese nation as well, has given the whole undertaking a strongly personal flavor. As conscious as the Japanese themselves of the tremendous drama of history, General MacArthur is the one great military figure of the recent conflict who has written his name on its pages in even larger letters in peace than he did in war.

[1] From Edwin O. Reischauer, *The United States and Japan* (Cambridge, Mass.: Harvard University Press, 1950), pp. 223–27. Copyright 1950 by the President and Fellows of Harvard College. Reprinted by permission of the publisher.

It will stand as one of the great names in Japanese history, surpassed by few in Japan's long annals and unrivaled by any since the stirring days of the Meiji period.

Few men who have found themselves in history's spotlight have better fitted the roles which destiny has given them than General MacArthur in his capacity as American proconsul in Japan and benevolent but absolute master of the fate of eighty million people. He has shown all the virtues which the Japanese admire. His strength of will rivals that of the strongest Japanese hero; his dignity and the firmness of his authority are all that they could hope for in their leaders; his austerity is only matched by his capacity for hard work; his insistence on strict obedience is paralleled by his own careful adherence to the orders which have governed his actions in Japan; even his insistence on unwavering personal loyalty on the part of his subordinates and his impatience with any form of criticism are qualities which the Japanese, with their own feeling for personal loyalty, understand and admire.

More important, General MacArthur provided the Japanese with the leadership and also the hope they so desperately needed in their hour of confusion and despair. Just when all hierarchy seemed to be crumbling, all discipline and will power melting away, and the individual Japanese was being cast adrift in the meaningless chaos into which society was disintegrating, there appeared from the least expected quarter a leader who with justness and determination began to create a new and presumably better order and put new purpose into life for the average Japanese. When things seemed blackest, he spoke out in ringing terms, giving a new hope to the Japanese and dignifying their suffering by pointing to the great historical advances to which it might lead. His flair for the dramatic, his thundering phrases, his appreciation of the tremendous historical significance of his own acts, all had a strong emotional appeal for the Japanese. Here was a leader who combined emotional depth with firmness of will.

General MacArthur became to the Japanese the symbol of perfection, the inspired leader, the knight in shining armor, and they repaid him, foreign conqueror though he was, with unlimited respect and often enough with adulation. His quick daily trips by car between his home in the former American Embassy and his headquarters in the Daiichi Building across the moat from the Emperor's burned-out palace in Tokyo drew crowds of admiring Japanese. They showered petitions upon him. While making him the personification of the power of the United States and regarding him as the sole source of all occupation policy, they also looked up to him as the prophet of the future Japan and their own national hero.

This is no time to make a final estimate of General MacArthur's unique role in postwar history. As one of America's principal wartime leaders, he has remained a somewhat controversial figure, and wartime attitudes toward him have often influenced personal judgments of his record in Japan. Some of his qualities are less admired by Americans than by Japanese. His insistence on personal loyalty and his intolerance of criticism have irritated American and Allied colleagues and subordinates far more than the Japanese. In the broad interpretations of his guiding instructions he has undoubtedly made some errors and shown certain blind spots. He has been subject to severe and sometimes justified attacks from various quarters, although the heavy cross fire from both right and left suggests that he has tended to remain not too far from the center of the road which he had been instructed to follow.

Certainly General MacArthur's role has not been so significant during the later years of the occupation as at first. As the Japanese, inspired by his strong stand, began to regain their self-confidence and to take hope in the prospect of a democratic Japan, they became less dependent upon him and his resounding phrases. This has been demonstrated by the gradual decline of popular interest in him in Japan. In time fewer Japanese than Americans gathered around the entrance of the Daiichi Building to watch him enter or leave. The respect remained, but the adulation was gone. It is even possible that some of the traits which had made General MacArthur a peerless leader in the first postwar years have become more of a hindrance than aid to the accomplishment of the objectives of the occupation. The development of responsible democratic leadership in Japan may well have been inhibited by General MacArthur's unchallenged authority and prestige, and his very greatness as a leader has perhaps helped to perpetuate Japanese habits of blind obedience to authority.

There can be no denying, however, that General MacArthur has been one of the great figures of the postwar world and may have accomplished more in Japan than any other man could have. Certainly none of the other leaders of occupation forces elsewhere in the world have accomplished proportionately as much, even in their more restricted tasks, and none of the men who were suggested at the end of the war as possible substitutes for General MacArthur had the combination of personal traits which fitted him so ideally for the post. Thus, as a great military hero in his own land and a still greater peace-time hero in the land he helped to conquer, his place among the great names of history is doubly secure.

29
William L. Neumann[1]

Professor Neumann's recent history of Japanese-American relations suggests that many of the achievements of Mac-Arthur and the Occupation were short-lived, and that some aims were undermined from the start by conflicting tendencies within SCAP.

General MacArthur and his aides viewed with suspicion men who had special knowledge of Japan and the Far East. The General disregarded almost completely the Far Eastern Commission of the Allied powers and paid little attention to the advisers and directives sent from Washington. He set about to democratize Japan with the help of the men he relied upon, men who had been trained in war and experienced in military operations rather than in government. If the Occupation had any comprehensive theory as a guide, it was that "what was good for the United States must be good for Japan."

The Meiji Constitution by which Japan had begun parliamentary government was put aside, and the Occupation authorities wrote a new constitution which was adopted by the Japanese Diet. Guarantees were provided for a number of democratic rights, including a free press and free speech. To prevent re-militarization an article was included in the constitution by which Japan renounced forever the right to make war and banned the maintenance of land, sea, and air forces.

The Occupation then functioned by means of directives which were dutifully incorporated into law by the Japanese Diet and carried out by the Prime Minister. By such means the police force was decentralized in the hope of preventing future political control; the same was done for the school system which had been so effectively used as a means of indoctrination. Large landholdings were broken up, and some effort made to curtail industrial combines and to collect reparations from the Japanese economy. Political parties along American models were strongly encouraged.

By the spring of 1947 General MacArthur and his aides could look

[1] From William L. Neumann, *America Encounters Japan: From Perry to Mac-Arthur* (Baltimore: Johns Hopkins Press, 1963), pp. 295–99. Reprinted by permission of the publisher.

back upon an imposing list of laws and decrees. The General thought
that he had completed his task and spoke of the spiritual revolution
which had taken place in Japan as "probably the greatest the world
had ever known." Democracy, he believed, was firmly implanted in
Japan, and this nation would henceforth be "the Switzerland of the
Pacific," MacArthur told newspapermen.

The Occupation continued, however, long after MacArthur believed that his work was completed due to the unwillingness of both
Stalin and Chiang Kai-shek to sign the peace treaty proposed by the
United States. The outbreak of the Korean War in the summer of
1950 turned the Pacific Commander to military tasks, and it was his
successors who saw the Occupation terminated in 1952, after President
Truman removed MacArthur from his post. The optimistic view of
American achievements in rebuilding Japan which characterized communiqués issued from Tokyo has remained the official version of the
seven years' accomplishments. When the Crown Prince and Crown
Princess visited Washington in September of 1960, President Eisenhower spoke of Japan as a proud country which "with us believes in
the democratic ideal of life." The President's gracious greeting ignored the fact that he had been prevented from paying an official
visit to Tokyo by anti-American riots in May and June which contrasted with his friendly reception in Seoul, Manila, and Taipeh.

It is too early to appraise the permanent effects of indirect American rule, but it also is obvious that the character of the changes in
Japan falls short of the official American and Japanese claims. If
Anglo-Saxon political institutions are transferable to another culture
they are slow to root and in growing take forms produced by mu-
tations. More than a century's effort at transplanting the North American political forms to Caribbean and Central American states strongly
suggests that it is very difficult if not impossible to disseminate the
Bill of Rights and the two-party system among peoples of radically
different cultures and living conditions.

Some of the Occupation's work has been undone since Japan re-
covered full sovereignty, while the Occupation itself retreated from
some of its goals before withdrawing. The primary influence in the
change of course was the growth of Russian-American and American-
Chinese antagonism. The first effect was to make Japan's Communists
and left wing parties, originally tolerated and even encouraged by the
Occupation, a threat to the model Japan which Americans hoped to
create. General MacArthur agreed to the curbing of some democratic
freedoms which were used excessively by the Communists; the Japa-

nese conservatives who dominated the post-Occupation governments went further. Civil servants and teachers, for example, had been guaranteed political freedom to prevent their becoming the helpless tools of the party in power. But when many of these individuals took part in Communist-led strikes and demonstrations, they found their freedom of political action withdrawn. Both the police system and the educational system have been recentralized since the restoration of sovereignty.

Some positive influences remain in effect. Many of the Occupation's critics grant that the American-sponsored land reform program went far in eliminating rural indebtedness and farm tenancy. Rural discontent was one of the major sources of the strength of the militarists. The change in the status of the Japanese woman also seems likely to remain one of the major accomplishments effected by the Occupation legislation and further facilitated in indirect ways by association with the thousands of lonely male Americans serving and working in Japan.

The presence of large numbers of Americans, both military and civilian, along with their dependents, may in time be seen to have exerted an even greater influence on Japan than the directives of the Supreme Commander. The mass culture of America—the juke box with its "pop tunes," television with its serials, the teenage set with its many fads—came to Japan. Those American cultural imports which existed in pre-war Japan were reinforced by the Occupation. Change also brought social disorganization; juvenile delinquency, theft, violence, sexual assault, which some of the older generation view as the evil products of Americanization and the destruction of traditional Japanese values. These complaints seem unlikely, however, to promote a successful purge of the imported elements which have fused in a variety of patterns with the indigenous culture.

One major goal of the Occupation, the creation of a neutral, unarmed nation without military leaders, has been almost completely discarded. The shift from a drastic demilitarization policy was begun by MacArthur. Faced with what seemed increasingly powerful Communist and Socialist demonstrations, the Occupation authorities began to fear an attempt at revolution. The Japanese government had only a minimal police force to protect itself and the Occupation leaders were hesitant about using American troops against Japanese civilians. General MacArthur agreed in 1950 to the establishment of a National Police Reserve of 75,000 men to cope with threatened subversion and public disorder. Trained and equipped initially by the American Army, this force soon rose to over 100,000 and drew its officers from the old Japanese Army. Renamed the National Security Force and expanding its arsenal of weapons to include tanks, this organization became the nucleus of a new army. Socialists challenged this development as a violation of the constitutional ban on armed forces, but the Japanese courts twice upheld the constitutionality of the new force.

30
Walter Millis[1]

In his study of civilian-military relations in the United States, the military historian, Walter Millis, has criticized MacArthur for introducing "political" considerations into a nonpolitical role. In this selection, Millis focuses upon MacArthur's activities in the early part of the Korean War.

Douglas MacArthur was a "political soldier"—a phenomenon comparatively rare in American experience, though by no means previously unknown. Because of the difference in backgrounds, the American political soldier has differed considerably from his European counterparts. We have never had a Cromwell to turn out a Parliament with bayonets or a Boulanger to act the man "on horseback." Because the military interest has never been a major institution in our state, we have never had a Waldersee or Ludendorff or Schleicher to assert the paramountcy of "the army" in political or diplomatic affairs. MacArthur never had "the Army" (much less the Navy or the Marines) behind him; he never spoke for a military interest as such, even though many military men were to agree with his positions, and there was never a time when he could be fairly compared to the European or Latin American political soldiers.

Yet he was a military politician. From an early date he had taken a close interest in partisan politics; he was prepared to use his prestige as a soldier to influence civil policy decisions, and the arguments of military necessity to override the diplomatic or political objectives of his civilian superiors. . . .

His was a complex, arrogant and forceful character. He was a military leader of indisputable ability, yet in his enormous reputation there was an element of propaganda myth, dating from the dark days of early 1942 when the American people had desperately needed a hero and MacArthur, defending Bataan, was the only figure available for the role. It can only have been galling to that proud personality. It may have intensified his natural egotism and sensitivity; his constant insistence upon the importance of the Far East as opposed to the European theater (where much less brilliant men, like

[1] From Walter Millis, *Arms and the State: Civil-Military Elements in National Policy* (New York: The Twentieth Century Fund, 1958), pp. 266–72.

Eisenhower or Bradley, were to earn greater laurels); his scorn of the politicians, and his almost compulsive drive to be always alone, supreme and unfettered.

This was the remarkable personality who presented what Forrestal, in the later stages of the Pacific war, once described as "the MacArthur problem." It was a problem with which most Washington staffs and administrators had long been familiar. Everybody knew that it had to be handled with gloves. Franklin Roosevelt had been adept at managing it; while the Truman State Department, alike under Marshall and Acheson, had experienced comparatively little difficulty with it during the long proconsulship in Japan. But fate now decreed that General MacArthur should become the chief executive agent of policies with which he did not agree, laid down by a Commander in Chief to whom he was politically opposed and whom he appears to have regarded with contempt. Something of the same kind had happened in the days of Lincoln and McClellan.

At the beginning, all went well so far as command relationships were concerned. The two divisions first deployed in Korea were swept back; but by late July a position was stabilized in the Pusan perimeter in the extreme southeast corner of the peninsula; reinforcements arrived; MacArthur reported that he now held "a secure base," and by August he was planning the brilliant counter-stroke at Inchon. MacArthur had to argue the Joint Chiefs into accepting this military gamble; but it seems fair to say that so far national policy, diplomacy, grand strategy and tactics in the theater had run in close harness. But now, with the immediate crisis apparently under control, issues of policy and politics raised an ugly head.

In the UN resolution of July 7, calling upon members to assist in repelling the aggression and to place their forces under the American UN commander, Chiang Kai-shek had seen an opportunity. The Generalissimo had offered 33,000 Chinese Nationalist troops to the common cause. MacArthur had agreed with the Joint Chiefs that it would be unwise to accept the offer. It was unlikely that these poorly trained and worse equipped formations would be "effective" in Korea; besides, they were needed to hold Formosa against a possible descent by the Chinese Communists. There were other considerations, of which State was particularly aware. One of the first decisions taken in the Blair House conferences was that Formosa should be neutralized. The United States had never before committed itself to defend Formosa against an attack from the mainland; now that it was about to do so by sending the 7th Fleet into Formosa Strait, it seemed essential to make it clear that we would not permit Formosa to be used as a base for a descent upon Communist China. To introduce Chinese Nationalist troops into Korea, where they would have a direct land approach into Manchuria, would vitiate this policy. The Chinese Communists were known to be extremely sensitive about Manchuria, where their position vis-à-vis the Russians was none too secure. Even in these early days, the possibility of a Chinese Communist intervention in the Korean War could not be disregarded. Nothing seemed more likely to invite it than the arrival of large Chinese Nationalist forces in the peninsula.

But the decisions of June 25 and 26 in Washington had made MacArthur, for the first time, responsible for the whole Far Eastern defense, including Formosa as well as Japan and Korea. Toward the end of July MacArthur informed Washington that he intended to inspect the Formosan addition to his command. JCS tried tactfully to suggest that since the State Department was dealing with the sensitive international problems of Formosa, MacArthur might prefer to send a senior staff officer to make the military survey rather than go himself. MacArthur brushed this idea aside, and visited the island on July 31.

According to his faithful aide, General Courtney Whitney, "It did not dawn on MacArthur that his visit to Formosa would be construed as being sinister in any way." Unfortunately, it dawned on nearly everybody else; and the world press immediately took the visit as an effort by MacArthur, if not by the United States, to revive the Chinese Nationalist forces as an instrument for a full-scale attack on Red China. This was not at all what our allies had had in mind in supporting our resistance to North Korean Communist aggression within the confines of Korea. MacArthur may have been as naive in this instance as Whitney represents him; but MacArthur was never a naive character. The reaction of the world press was fairly violent, and on August 5 Louis Johnson dispatched a directive instructing MacArthur once more that United States policy was both to protect Formosa against Communist attack and to prevent any attack upon the mainland by the Generalissimo. MacArthur answered that he "understood" and would be governed "meticulously" by the directive. But the Administration was uneasy. It dispatched Averell Harriman, as special representative of the President, in the hope of arriving at a better understanding.

Harriman reached Tokyo on August 6 and had several long sessions with the Commander in Chief Far East (CINCFE). "For reasons," he reported, "which are rather difficult to explain, I did not feel that we came to a full agreement on the way we believed things should be handled on Formosa and with the Generalissimo. He accepted the President's position and will act accordingly, but without full conviction. He has a strange idea that we should back anybody who will fight communism, even though he could not give an argument why the Generalissimo's fighting Communists would be a contribution towards the effective dealing with the Communists in China." MacArthur made the rather pointed suggestion that he was "prepared to deal with the policy problems," but added that he would "conscientiously deal only with the military side unless he is given further orders from the President." It was an early sign of a dangerous ambiguity in the situation. Through the four and a half years of his rule in Japan, MacArthur had combined the functions of a five-star general with those of the principal American political officer in the Far East. His experience and position entitled him to "deal with the policy problems"; what it did not entitle him to do was to control policy issues in the guise of giving "purely military" advice.

The newspapers were now interpreting MacArthur's visit to Formosa as a sign that the general had "rejected" the President's policy of neutralizing the island. Since MacArthur had privately agreed to be good and go along, Truman issued a statement that he and the general "saw eye to eye on the Formosa problem." Naturally, this only created more hostility between two forceful personalities who were actually seeing eye to eye on almost nothing. On August 10 MacArthur issued a scorching declaration on his visit to Formosa:

> This visit has been maliciously misrepresented to the public by those who invariably in the past have propagandized a policy of defeatism and appeasement in the Pacific. I hope the American people will not be misled by sly insinuations, brash speculations and bold misstatements invariably attributed to anonymous sources, so insidiously fed them both nationally and internationally by persons 10,000 miles away from the actual events, if they are not indeed designed, to promote disunity and destroy faith and confidence in American purposes and institutions and American representatives at this time of great world peril.

Though elusively worded, like so many MacArthur statements, it sounded very much like an accusation of defeatism and appeasement against the Truman Administration; at the very least, it seemed to represent a claim by MacArthur to comparable authority with Truman's in the development of Far Eastern policy. Clearly, there were rifts ahead.

The military position, on the other hand, seemed increasingly hopeful. While UN forces had been compressed into a perilously narrow perimeter around Taegu and Pusan (in the extreme southeastern corner of the peninsula), they were holding and reinforcements were arriving. The 24th, 25th and 1st Cavalry Divisions from Japan were in Korea; the 1st Marine Division, representing the initial reinforcement from the United States, had begun to arrive on August 2. By mid-August MacArthur was concerting his plans for a counter-attack. At this moment an invitation arrived in the Tokyo headquarters to prepare a message for the annual convention of the Veterans of Foreign Wars. A theater commander in the full tide of dangerous action is scarcely required to respond to such requests. But "MacArthur decided," in the somewhat incredible words of Whitney, "that this was an excellent opportunity to place himself on record as being squarely behind the President."

His method of doing so was curious. The message to the VFW carried several implied barbs for Administration policy. "Nothing could be more fallacious than the threadbare argument by those who advocate appeasement and defeatism in the Pacific that if we defend Formosa we alienate continental Asia." At the moment, Tokyo dispatches were quoting "reliable sources" to the effect that MacArthur felt that the United States should "take more aggressive action against communism not only in Korea but elsewhere in Asia." Our UN allies were already nervous over the idea that the Korean police action might be expanded into a general crusade against communism in the Far East that would precipitate the third world war. Before the United Nations, the Soviet Union was resoundingly accusing us of "aggression," not only in Korea but because of our alleged designs on Formosa; the MacArthur message could be (as later it was) used as powerful ammunition in this propaganda war. Truman first saw it on August 26, two days before its intended release. He has later said that he thought then of relieving the general. The matter was so serious that he summoned the Secretaries of State and Defense, the Joint Chiefs and Secretary of the Treasury John W. Snyder. They were all "shocked," but apparently none dared at that point to suggest the relief of the towering figure of the Commander in Chief Far East. Instead, the President instructed Johnson to send him a message directing that he "withdraw" the statement. Truman knew that it was already in type (in the *U.S. News and World Report*) and so could not be suppressed; the withdrawal order was intended simply to limit the damage, so far as possible, by making it clear that Mac-Arthur was not speaking for the Administration.

According to Whitney, MacArthur was "utterly astonished." He withdrew the statement in an abrupt telegram of acquiescence; but began to see himself the victim of conspiracy. In the eyes of the Tokyo headquarters it seemed "logical," again according to Whitney, that the VFW statement had "innocently" run afoul of "plans being hatched in the State Department to succumb to British pressure and desert the Nationalist Government on Formosa. . . . in the event that the State Department was conspiring with the British to hand over Formosa to the Communists, it is easy to see how the statement to the VFW would cause consternation." Here, as elsewhere, it is difficult to know how accurately General Whitney, writing after the event, represents the state of mind obtaining in Tokyo at the time. If his report is trustworthy, it would seem to indicate that already an impossible situation had developed between the Commander in Chief Far East and his superiors, both military and political, in Washington. The episode, says Whitney, gave MacArthur "his first clear illustration of the devious workings of the Washington-London team." A theater commander in wartime who really believed that the civil authorities were "conspiring" against him with a foreign power would surely be compelled to resign. But MacArthur did not resign; and the issue passed.

31

D. F. Fleming[1]

One of MacArthur's most virulent critics is the diplomatic historian, D. F. Fleming. Fleming's massive study, The Cold War and Its Origins, *is one of the pioneering "revisionist" histories of the Cold War, and MacArthur figures prominently as a leading warhawk. In this selection, he reproves MacArthur for deliberately sabotaging peace efforts during the Korean War.*

On October 15 President Truman flew to Wake Island for a conference with General MacArthur, taking with him a large staff of his experts. Given a choice of meeting the President at Wake Island or at Honolulu, far to the West, MacArthur chose Wake. The General was a little late in meeting the President's plane and he chose to shake the hand of his Commander-in-Chief instead of saluting him. MacArthur had come reluctantly and the conference ended hours ahead of schedule, the General being preoccupied and impatient to return to Tokyo.

In this conference the General told the President that resistance would end in North Korea by Thanksgiving. When asked about the chances of Soviet or Chinese interference, MacArthur replied: "Very little." In the first or second months their intervention would have been decisive. Now it was no longer feared. If they tried, the Chinese could only get "50,000 to 60,000" men across the Yalu River and "if the Chinese tried to get down to Pyongyang there would be the greatest slaughter."

At the time MacArthur made these statements to the President he knew, from many sources, that the Chinese were already in North Korea in force.

. . . This information had come from Nationalist quarters on Formosa, British Intelligence at Hong Kong and from Koreans parachuted along the Yalu who had walked back through the enemy lines.

MacArthur deceived the President in this vital matter because he feared that his plan for an offensive to the Yalu might be vetoed. Nor did the President have any success in convincing him that "com-

[1] From D. F. Fleming, *The Cold War and Its Origins* (London: George Allen & Unwin Ltd., 1961), vol. 2, pp. 617–22, 634–38. Reprinted by permission of Doubleday & Company, Inc.

munism, especially in China, cannot be overcome by armed force."

On returning to Tokyo MacArthur promptly issued a statement favoring the proclamation of a "Pacific Doctrine" which would re-affirm American determination to give assistance to any nation in the Far East, threatened from within or without by Soviet Communism.

Naturally there was no meeting of minds about Formosa. When he returned to Tokyo MacArthur issued a statement saying: "It is known here that General MacArthur holds unalterably to the view that Formosa should not be allowed to fall into the hands of a potential enemy of the free nations of the Pacific." This led the President to say at his press conference that "Formosa was settled a month ago, or five weeks ago, and there was nothing about Formosa to be settled with General MacArthur." . . .

MacArthur had had instructions from the Joint Chiefs of Staff not to use anything but South Koreans near the Manchurian frontier, but on October 24 he lifted these restrictions, without consulting Washington, and enjoined his commanders to drive forward with all speed, utilizing all their forces. On the same day the Joint Chiefs called his attention to the violations of his instructions and he replied on the 25th that the Korean troops were not of sufficient strength or well enough led. It was "military necessity" to use his American forces. General Lawton Collins, Chief of Staff of the Army, did not believe that these arguments were valid, or that there was any reason why MacArthur could not consult the Joint Chiefs of Staff and ask for a change in his instructions. . . .

In Korea the UN forces continued their advance northward. The Joint Chiefs of Staff had reluctantly sanctioned MacArthur's violation of his instructions not to send American troops near the Manchurian or Soviet frontiers, but they continued to try to keep them some distance back. On November 24 the JCS advised MacArthur about the growing concern of the other members of the UN over the danger of a general war if his forces approached the frontiers too closely and suggested five cautionary measures, among them that he should not send his forces down to the Yalu River, but hold these forces, principally South Koreans, in the hills "dominating the approaches to the valley." He was also advised that the UN forces "continue to make every effort to spare hydroelectric installations" and that "the ultimate handling of the extremely sensitive Northeast province (fronting the Soviet Union) would await UN procedures."

In his reply the next day MacArthur rejected all of these procedures as "provocative of the very consequence" the JCS were seeking to avoid. It was necessary to destroy all North Korean forces and it would be "utterly impossible to stop on the commanding terrain south of the Yalu, as suggested. As for the hydroelectric installations that "would not be a major factor, either to the Chinese Communists or to the Soviets." After he had consolidated his position on the Yalu he would use South Korean troops there, "as far as possible."

Four days earlier, on October 21, MacArthur had announced: "the war is very definitely coming to an end shortly. It looks as if we have closed the trap."

Early in November his reports indicated contact with "a fresh enemy force" and on November 5 strong Chinese forces struck at the same time that a broadcast in Peking rallied the Chinese people.

After the first setback from Chinese forces, "abrupt calm" developed on the battlefront. Britain strongly urged the United States to permit the Chinese to occupy a buffer zone. Dispatches from Moscow on November 14 related that the Chinese intended to drive the U.S. forces out of Korea, and on the 16th China sent a message to the United Nations justifying its right to help North Korea resist "American aggression" and vowing to fight until it was ended. On the same day Defense Minister Emanuel Shinwell told the British House of Commons that Britain was seeking in consultations with other governments to bring the hostilities to an early conclusion and "to limit their extent." Churchill supported this endeavor. On November 22, "well informed sources" in Washington indicated that agreement on a plan for a buffer strip along the Manchurian border was near and awaited "primarily approval of its military details by General of the Army Douglas MacArthur." Final agreement was expected momentarily.

MacArthur gave his answer to these efforts to end the war by flying to the front and launching 100,000 men toward the Yalu River in two giant encircling movements which if successful "should for all practical purposes end the war." Informally, he called it a "home by Christmas" offensive. His two wings were so far apart that it was difficult to establish any liaison between them and none was attempted except through Tokyo. . . .

The Chinese forces quickly entered the huge gap between the two UN armies and turned general assault into headlong retreat, bringing also a storm of criticism upon MacArthur from our European allies. Delegates at Lake Success wanted to know why he should launch an offensive just on the eve of the arrival of the delegation of Chinese communists at Lake Success. The French Government felt that he had possibly "launched his offensive at this time to wreck the negotiations by the French and the British for a settlement of the frontier issue with the Chinese Communists." The British *New Statesman and Nation* declared that MacArthur had "acted in defiance of all common sense, and in such a way as to provoke the most peace loving nation." . . .

A responsible American writer, McGeorge Bundy, went further and plainly labelled MacArthur as a provocator. Neither our own policy nor that of the UN required his dash to the Manchurian border "and this MacArthur knew. . . . The decision was his; it was provocation." . . .

The *New York Herald Tribune* underlined editorially the deliberate nature of the blunder in an editorial headed "MacArthur's Disaster." When a Chinese attack suddenly unhinged his army's advance in early November he had issued a dramatic communique complaining that the Communists had "committed one of the most offensive acts of international lawlessness of historic record." Continuing, MacArthur had said that "a possible trap was surreptitiously laid calculated to encompass the destruction of the UN forces." Then, said the editor, "Just nineteen days later General MacArthur walked directly into the trap he had described." It was "difficult to put confidence in the military capacity of a headquarters which has so gravely compounded blunder by confusion of facts and intelligence."

One of two conclusions was inescapable. Either MacArthur was a highly incompetent military commander, or he was deliberately trying to extend the war into a conflict with China.

Confronted by disaster MacArthur denied he had meant the home by Christmas part seriously. He declared that the United Nations faced "an entirely new war" and called upon it for "a solution," a remark which many regarded as a proposal to carry the war to China. . . .

After two months more of fighting, General MacArthur visited the Korean battlefield, on March 7, and issued a statement saying that a stalemate was indicated, assuming "a continuation of the existing limitation on our freedom of counter-offensive action." A few days later, General Ridgway, who had largely superseded MacArthur as the actual commander in Korea, declared that if the war ended with UN troops at the 38th Parallel he would consider the result "a tremendous victory." . . .

. . . The idea of stopping the war around the 38th was attractive to Lake Success. On March 13 UN diplomats reported that the idea of unifying Korea by military victory was being quietly dropped. More and more Western delegates were saying that the restoration of peace and security "in the area," meant South Korea, not the whole country.

Unless something were done it seemed apparent that a stalemate was going to be accepted. The issue was acute also because the UN forces were approaching the 38th Parallel again. The situation was ripe for some diplomatic initiative. . . .

Behind the scenes a serious effort was being made to work out an overture to the Chinese which might stop the war. It was to take the form of a public statement by President Truman and the text was being circulated to the governments of the 13 UN members which had troops in Korea.

The proposed statement pointed out that "the aggressors" in Korea had been driven

> back to the general vicinity from which the unlawful attack was first launched and that, therefore, the principal objective of repelling North Korean and Chinese Communist aggression against the South Korean Republic had been achieved.
>
> It asserted that further United Nations objectives, such as unification and the establishment of a free government in all of Korea, could and should be accomplished without further fighting or blood-shed.
>
> The Chinese Communists were, in effect, given an invitation to cease fire and to agree to a settlement of outstanding issues by negotiation.

The proposal did not openly abandon the objective of a united, Western-controlled Korea, but it practically did so by suggesting an end to the fighting when it was near the 38th. Peace by negotiation, instead of by unconditional surrender and victory, was plainly offered. It was to be a real peace including "the peaceful settlement of other problems, as is envisaged in the Charter of the United Nations." China would have a good chance of gaining her seat in the UN and of recovering Formosa, even from the Western majority, since in both cases the long term logic was on her side. For its part, the authority of the UN would be vindicated and maintained, an epochal gain in world history.

While this hopeful solution of an essentially stalemated situation was being canvassed among the 13 Allies, the Joint Chiefs of Staff sent a dispatch to MacArthur, on March 20, 1951, which said

> State planning a Presidential announcement shortly that with clearing of bulk of South Korea of aggressors, United Nations now pre-

pared to discuss conditions of settlement in Korea. United Nations feeling exists that further diplomatic efforts toward settlement should be made before any advance with major forces north of the thirty-eighth parallel. Time will be required to determine diplomatic reactions and permit new negotiations that may develop. . . . .

This was plainly one of the most important messages ever sent to the military headquarters of the UN in Tokyo. . . .

Four days after he received this vitally important message, Mac-Arthur issued a cease-fire proposal of his own, in terms that were certain to be rejected. His message to the enemy explained in detail how Red China had failed on the battlefield, how it lacked the industrial capacity to provide the critical items necessary to the conduct of modern war, how with the "development of existing methods of mass destruction" China's numbers could not win. Therefore the enemy must be "painfully aware that a decision of the United Nations to depart from its tolerant effort to contain the war to the area of Korea," by bombing and blockading China, would doom her "to the risk of imminent military collapse."

After this threat, which he had absolutely no authority to make, MacArthur went on to say that he stood ready to "confer in the field with the commander-in-chief of the enemy forces in an earnest effort to find any military means whereby the realization of the political objectives of the United Nations" might be accomplished.

In other words, if the Chinese would confess themselves licked, the Supreme Commander would accept their surrender, though it was not the Chinese who were proposing a cease-fire. Knowing well that he was meddling in politics, MacArthur was careful to talk about "military means" of achieving the UN's objectives, meaning the unification of Korea under our auspices. The "military means" of doing this were, obviously, not an armistice in the field but a vast expansion of the war. MacArthur toured the battlefield after his statement, making it plain to the newspapermen that he did not intend to let the Chinese regroup above the 38th.

The General had completely torpedoed the effort of the United States and the United Nations to bring the slaughter in Korea to an end. Peking spurned the MacArthur "offer" as an insolent ultimatum, not justified by military events, and there was nothing to do but abandon the UN's effort to stop the war. Marshall said later:

> At the time the foregoing statement was issued the clearance of the proposed Presidential declaration with the other thirteen nations having

forces in Korea had very nearly been completed. In view of the serious impact of General MacArthur's statement on the negotiations with these nations, it became necessary to abandon the effort, thus losing whatever chance there may have been at that time to negotiate a settlement of the Korean conflict.

In his defense MacArthur admitted that he had received the JCS message of March 20, but he asserted that "it had nothing whatever to do with my statement, though. The President is constantly, as I understand it, engaged in methods to try to bring the thing to an end, and the message I received hadn't the slightest bearing upon the statement I put out, which was a military appraisal, my military appraisal of the situation, and my offer to meet the commander-in-chief to discuss peace terms." He had done it twice before, MacArthur continued, and "there is nothing unusual or unorthodox or improper that I can possibly read into the statement I made. . . ."

Questioned by Senator Morse, MacArthur said that the message of March 20 to him was "merely normal." The "purpose of the message was to find out what modifications might be necessary in limiting our advances north."

This is perhaps the classic example of a general grown so great that nothing which the President of the United States or the United Nations did meant anything to him. He was willing for the President to be busy "constantly" trying "to bring the thing to an end." It didn't matter to MacArthur, or doubtless to legions of his worshippers, but his brush-off of the President and the UN did not pass with his military colleagues and superiors. Marshall agreed with the statement that MacArthur "jumped the gun," putting us "again" in the position of speaking "with two voices" and said that "it should have been evident to him that that would very seriously complicate, if not terminate at that time," the President's effort as "the executive agent of the United Nations."

Bradley testified "I certainly would not have issued any such statement under those circumstances." Collins said that MacArthur "had been clearly notified" by the JCS that the President intended to speak very shortly and "he thereby as a field commander did something that a field commander ought not to do with respect to a proposed statement by his Commander-in-Chief." One or two parts of the two statements were so similar that Admiral Sherman wondered if MacArthur had obtained a text of the President's proposed statement through one of the 13 nations concerned, but General Vandenberg held that "whether the text had been sent or not would have made very little difference to me." He would either have cleared his armistice statement or waited for more information, and General Wedemeyer, who was very sympathetic to MacArthur, agreed that MacArthur "should have communicated with his commander-in-chief in advance of offering terms of surrender in the field."

Later MacArthur came close to admitting in a speech to the American Legion that he had deliberately torpedoed the President's effort to stop the war. There was, he said, "little doubt that the yielding of Formosa and the seating of China in the United Nations was fully planned when I called upon the enemy commander in Korea on March 24 to meet me in the field to arrange armistice terms." He had "unquestionably wrecked the secret plan to yield on these issues as the price for peace in Korea." Then "there followed the violent Washington reaction against me for what was actually so normal a military move."

32
John W. Spanier[1]

In his account of the Truman-MacArthur controversy, political scientist John W. Spanier found MacArthur's strategic policy formulations to have considerable consistency and some merit. On the other hand, he contended that the general's political role and insubordinate performance left Truman, as the nation's civilian spokesman, no alternative but to fire him.

MacArthur's fundamental charge against the Administration was that its restrictions kept him from achieving "victory" in the field. Inherent in this accusation was MacArthur's repudiation of the Administration's basic assumptions, above all the supposition that the Soviet Union might be ready and willing to fight a total war, and that the United States, therefore, must not provide an eager Kremlin with any excuse for attack.

MacArthur contended that the Administration divorced theory from practice. In theory, American foreign policy was based upon the assumption that the United States held sufficient power, above all air-atomic striking power, to deter the Soviet Union from launching an all-out war; in practice, American policy-makers acted upon the assumption that a limited extension of the war would hand the Soviets an excuse for precipitating World War III. On the one hand, the Kremlin was allegedly reluctant to engage in global hostilities with the United States because of America's greater retaliatory strength, inherent primarily in the destructive power of the Strategic Air Command; on the other hand, the Kremlin regarded our purported deterrent power with so little respect that it would deliberately risk total war rather than suffer a limited defeat of Communist China (a limited defeat would preclude the unconditional surrender and overthrow of Peking, and leave it weakened but nevertheless in control of the Chinese mainland).

MacArthur failed to see any consistency between the Administration's rationale of its foreign policy, based upon the atomic impact of massive retaliation, and its failure to act upon its own premise. If

[1] From John W. Spanier, *The Truman-MacArthur Controversy and the Korean War* (Cambridge, Mass.: The Belknap Press of Harvard University Press, 1959), pp. 262–68. Copyright 1959 by the President and Fellows of Harvard College. Reprinted by permission of the publisher.

it were true that the United States held the atomic balance—as he believed and the Administration professed—then his recommendations for air attacks and a naval blockade of Communist China could be safely executed. SAC would continue to deter the Soviet Union and ensure that the limited hostilities, although somewhat extended, would remain confined to the Chinese-Korean theater; our superior strategic air power would provide the umbrella under which this expanded limited war could be fought. It was sheer fantasy, MacArthur charged, to suppose that American air attacks upon Manchuria would provide an eager Kremlin the opportunity to enter the battle. The Soviet Union possessed far inferior retaliatory power (the Russians did not begin to develop their long-range air force until 1954); why should it, therefore, be allowed to handcuff American strength? The United States possessed the superior atomic sanction; why should it not take advantage of this greater power? MacArthur pointed to the paradox that the side with the smaller strategic strength had paralyzed the will to act of the side which possessed the more effective striking force. The Administration's fear to act upon his recommendations to attack across the Yalu and the resultant impasse on the Korean battlefield was not a military stalemate, but a stalemate between the Soviet leaders *militarily incapable* of destroying the center of free world power and American policy-makers *psychologically reluctant* to exploit the advantage of the very atomic balance which they claimed was the primary safeguard of peace.

If the Russian leaders were really militarily capable of winning a total war and were merely seeking a convenient pretext to launch World War III, they would hardly need the United States to furnish the excuse; they were perfectly capable of manufacturing their own. If they were, however, restrained by American air power, they would rather tolerate a limited defeat of their chief ally than risk suicide. North Korea was no more "worth" the cost of an all-out conflict to the Soviet Union than South Korea had been to the United States; nor was Communist China's position in North Korea "worth" that price as long as American objectives remained confined to the Korean peninsula.

MacArthur also dissented from the Administration's assumption that even if an attack upon Communist China would not precipitate World War III, this country must not become engaged in a "war of attrition" lest this course would weaken NATO and provoke a Soviet attack. The General denied that the Korean War was a Russian maneuver to draw American strength away from Europe and dissipate it against Chinese manpower, a strategic diversion which must be ended as soon as possible at minimum cost to the central effort to strengthen our total-war deterrent.

Not only was the "real" challenge against the enemy's number-one team in Europe hypothetical, for it was "Russia's policy . . . not to sacrifice its own troops but to use those of friends," but:

> Mr. Truman failed abysmally to comprehend the Soviet Strategy in the latter's continuing and relentless effort to control the world . . . He failed to understand that the global panorama has long encompassed three great areas of potential struggle: In the center, Europe; on the flanks, Asia to the north and Africa to the south. Mr. Truman apparently thought of the center as the area of supreme interest and potential struggle, believing that if it could be held safely all else would fall into place. . . .
>
> What the Soviets sought were the economic frontiers of the world—Asia to the north, Africa to the south—frontiers which possessed such a mighty reservoir of the world's potential wealth in raw resources. The center represented little in economic advance, the flanks everything. The Soviet strategy was merely to defend in Europe but to advance by way of the flanks; to cause the free world to concentrate its resources at the center to the neglect of the vital ends.

Korea was, therefore, the right war at the right place at the right time, and above all else, with the right enemy. For Communist China was Soviet Russia's chief ally and most powerful friend in Asia. Therefore, a defeat inflicted upon Communist China, however limited that defeat might be, would affect both Soviet strength in Asia and the global balance of power between the Western and Communist blocs. The defeat of the Chinese Communists in Korea would strengthen the friendship and support of the Asian peoples, particularly the Japanese and Filipinos, for the United States; the loss of American prestige in an acceptance of the stalemate would alienate their sympathies. Conversely, Communist China's status would be recognized as "the military colossus of the East"; America's fear to demonstrate its superior strength would make our friends feel less secure and drive the neutral nations deeper into neutralism; for they would feel more threatened as a result of Peking's unchallenged recognition as a strong and menacing neighbor and therefore look upon the Communist states with a more friendly, if also a more apprehensive, eye. The destruction of Communist China's industrial complex, military depots, and communication network would gravely weaken Sino-Soviet offensive strength in the Far East and deter Moscow and Peking from initiating any further aggressive adventures; confining hostilities to the Korean peninsula and concluding the war on the basis of the *status quo* would leave Sino-Soviet power intact and encourage it to exploit the West's weakness and lack of determination in other areas. Indeed, if the war in Korea were "lost"—by MacArthur's definition—the Western democracies would have suffered such a first-class political and psychological defeat that the Soviets could not but be emboldened to new efforts to undermine Western Europe. But to drive the Chinese Communists out of Korea in accordance with his strategy, MacArthur asserted, would demonstrate to the Western nations that even the Sino-Soviet alliance shrank from certain risky steps; victory would raise Europe's self-confidence by showing the limits of Communist power and the superior strength of the United States. It is for this reason that MacArthur insisted that Korea was *the* test of NATO and that Europe's first line of defense was not in Germany but in Korea.

His war in Korea was not, therefore, a sideshow; it was at the center of the world-wide struggle. The war, to be sure, contained its risks, but this was inherent in the nature of international politics and the original decision to fight in Korea; the conflict also presented a great opportunity to inflict a limited yet severe defeat upon the Sino-Soviet block, demonstrate American determination and power, raise Western resolution and self-assurance, and forestall the disaffection of friendly Asian nations. This opportunity outweighed all the risks, particularly since these risks were minimized by the deterrent power of America's superior atomic air-striking power.

MacArthur also emphasized that an alliance could act decisively only if its members were agreed on the nature of the danger facing them. If they were not animated by such a common realization, they not only did not add to the security of the United States; they detracted from it by restraining the United States from taking the steps necessary to safeguard its interests. The argument that the Administration could not accept his recommendations because it could not afford to isolate itself in the face of the Soviet threat toward Europe, was invalid; it was not the existence of the alliance which would deter the enemy's aggression, but the resolution which bound it together in concrete instances which called for vigorous action. When such determination and will-power were lacking, the United States must protect its own interests. The Administration's unwillingness to risk the loss of its allies allowed American policy to be dictated by the weaker members of the alliance. Under these circumstances, the achievement of allied unity became self-defeating; for the price of continued cooperation was the substance of action. In MacArthur's opinion, this price was too high and was paid upon the false assumption that unilateral action by the United States in Asia woud undermine NATO, isolate this country, and encourage a Soviet attack in Europe. MacArthur believed that this prejudged the issue because it presumed that the United States was more dependent for its security upon its European allies than they upon the United States.

Since he was unwilling to accept formal unity for inaction or halfhearted effort, MacArthur advised that in order to forestall the disastrous effects he foresaw from an acceptance of a Korean stalemate, the United States "go it alone." European reluctance to become involved in major hostilities in the Far East ought not to prevent the Administration from taking actions which were in America's interest; the Administration could not give global scope to an alliance whose conflict of interests in areas outside of Europe paralyzed it.

The United States was sufficiently strong to fight the Korean War by herself; she had to act unilaterally if necessary, and pursue alone those policies which aimed at the preservation of a favorable balance of power. The United States must not allow this balance to be overturned by subordinating her strategy to allied fears; for in the final analysis, the security of Europe depended upon this country's ability to maintain this equilibrium. After the North Korean invasion, the United States had not first asked its allies whether they would approve of American intervention; the American government had acted in accordance with the dictates of national security. Allied consent had subsequently been extended, but it had not been a precondition for action. The Administration ought now to act upon its own precedent.

Communist China's appearance on the battlefield thus brought into the open the almost total disagreement between the Administration and its Commander in Chief, Far East, a disagreement which had, of course, never lain far below the surface and had irritated the relationship between Washington and Tokyo from the beginning of the war. Since shortly after the outbreak of hostilities, MacArthur had openly advocated that the United States maximize its commitment to Chiang Kai-shek and take a strong stand against Communist China; and his repeated "military" criticisms of the Administration's preoccupation with Europe and alleged neglect of American interests in the Far East were hardly new.

But these frequent and vigorous challenges of Administration policy after China's intervention were, however, incompatible with the President's continuing civilian supremacy and authority as chief diplomat and Commander in Chief to formulate and implement the policies the Chief Executive considered necessary to ensure the nation's self preservation. MacArthur embarrassed the Administration by giving the world the impression that the United States spoke with two voices—one civilian, one military—on foreign policy; he confused our allies and increased their reluctance to follow American policy because they feared that the government could not control him and his March 24 statement actually forestalled the execution of Presidential policy. This situation was intolerable and left Mr. Truman no choice but to dismiss his field commander. But the price the President paid included, among other things, the adoption of a stronger anti-Mao and pro-Chiang policy along the lines advocated by the "old soldier" who refused to fade away.

33
Samuel P. Huntington[1]

> *Political scientist Samuel P. Huntington continued the critical scholarly evaluation of MacArthur when he discussed the general's ideas in* The Soldier and the State. *For Huntington, however, the problem with MacArthur was not that he embodied the values of the career officer class, but that he was not "professional" enough. MacArthur, unlike most military men, held liberal views on war and peace, Huntington maintained, and these, rather than his militarism, caused his difficulties with civilian authority.*

From the start, MacArthur had been a brilliant soldier but always something more than a soldier: a controversial, ambitious, transcendent figure, too able, too assured, too talented to be confined within the limits of professional function and responsibility. As early as 1929 his name was mentioned in connection with the Presidency, and in 1944, 1948, and 1952 he was on the fringes of the presidential political arena. The MacArthur ideology which evolved in the 1920's and 1930's was essentially religious, mystical, and emotional, contrasted with the normally practical, realistic, and materialistic approach of the professional soldier. To an even greater extent than Mahan, MacArthur's attitudes appeared to reflect a deeply felt and profoundly personalized version of Christianity. In contrast to the professional stress on military force in being, he emphasized the moral and spiritual aspects of war and the importance of the citizen-soldier. In contrast to the bulk of the officer corps, MacArthur viewed the threats to the United States as arising from insidious political philosophies rather than from other nation states of equal or superior material strength. His sense of mission and dedication gave rise to a sustained and unbridled optimism which contrasted with the normal professional pessimism. The professional officer exists in a world of grays. MacArthur's universe was one of blacks and whites and loud and clashing colors. His articulate and varying views reflected a continuing quest for beliefs and policies which

[1] From Samuel P. Huntington, *The Soldier and the State: The Theory of Civil-Military Relations* (Cambridge, Mass.: The Belknap Press of Harvard University Press, 1957), pp. 369–72. Copyright 1957 by the President and Fellows of Harvard College. Reprinted by permission of the publisher.

would satisfy his own ideological inclinations and at the same time inspire favorable popular response. . . .

From an early period MacArthur's attitude toward war embodied the dominant ideas of the American liberal tradition. During the 1920's and 1930's he had justified war on moral and religious grounds, and surrounded the warrior's art with a sentimental romanticism. Unlike Dennis Hart Mahan, but similar to Mahan's Jacksonian opponents, MacArthur preferred the warlike spirit to the military spirit. Some observers detected irony many years later in 1951 and 1952, when MacArthur denounced the dangers of the "military mind." But the general was on firm ground. A vast gulf existed between his thinking and that of the professional officer. After World War II he adopted the pacifist ideas which he had castigated in the 1920's and 1930's, urging in Kellogg-Briand terms that war must be "outlawed from the world." Seldom has a professionally trained military man more completely departed from the cardinal tenet of military doctrine that war is ultimately inevitable and beyond the power of humans to prevent. MacArthur had the ban on the maintenance of armed forces written into the constitution of Japan. He urged his own nation to "proclaim our readiness to abolish war in concert with the great powers of the world." MacArthur's demand for the total abolition of war reflected his unwillingness to accept the frustrations, embarrassment, and burdens of continued international friction. In Lasswellian phrases he declared that "in final analysis the mounting cost of preparation for war is in many ways as materially destructive as war itself." Instead he turned to the abolition of war as the panacea of the world's ills, "the one issue, which, if settled, might settle all others." Despite their differences, an underlying consistency existed between MacArthur's earlier and later views on war. War was always a total, cataclysmic act. In his earlier years he stressed the heroic self-sacrifice and glory involved in this act. In his later years he saw the destruction and calamity it entailed. But his reactions to war were always extreme. "You cannot control war; you can only abolish it," he declared, rejecting vigorously the concept that "when you use force, you can limit that force." Adherence to the total war-total peace dichotomy necessarily led MacArthur to a theory of civil-military relations closer to Ludendorff than to Clausewitz. War represented the utter bankruptcy of politics, not simply the extension of politics. Consequently, in war full control, "politically, economically, militarily," must be in the hands of the military commanders, and the nation must concentrate its complete trust in the military leadership.

34

Louis Morton[1]

MacArthur's Reminiscences, *written shortly before his death in 1964 and published shortly thereafter, quickly became the nation's number one best-seller. To scholars, the book revealed a good deal about MacArthur's character and views, as indicated by this penetrating review by military historian Louis Morton.*

When, on August 21, 1963, it was revealed that General MacArthur had at last written his autobiography, the news was greeted in some quarters as the promise of a publication event of the first magnitude. For years the General had resisted offers to write a book or to take advantage of an open invitation by the Army to publish his report of operations in World War II and the Occupation of Japan. As a matter of fact, this report, in the form of an oversized and elaborately illustrated three-volume history, had already been completed (and printed in five copies) before he left Tokyo in 1951. But by arrangement with MacArthur, it had not been published and access to it had been restricted to official users.

Announcement of the autobiography had somewhat the nature of a revelation. All 220,000 words of it, we were told, had been written over a period of six months in the General's own hand on fourteen-inch yellow pads. General Courtney Whitney had "caught him" at it and passed the word to Henry Luce, who immediately made arrangements for serial publication in *Life.* Ranking the *Reminiscences* with the greatest historical writings of any age, Mr. Luce declared, "The General is as clearly a master of narrative and language as he is of strategy and statesmanship."

If MacArthur's reputation as a strategist and statesman rested on the *Reminiscences,* the task of the historian would be relatively simple, for MacArthur is certainly not a "master of narrative and language." But the problem is more complex. The fact is that here, as in everything else involving MacArthur, we are faced with a contradiction. The General's talents were considerable and his contribution in peace

[1] From Louis Morton, "Egotist in Uniform," *Harper's Magazine* 229 (November, 1964): 138, 142, 144–45. Copyright © 1964 by Harper's Magazine, Inc. Reprinted from the November, 1964 issue of *Harper's Magazine* by permission of the author.

and war undeniably large. But he had serious weaknesses, and many of his actions were not above criticism. He had the capacity to inspire both love and hate, admiration and fear. He had a strong personality, a flamboyant style, great moral and physical courage, a high sense of patriotism and duty, and a profound belief in his own destiny. But he was also a supreme egotist who could brook no criticism. He seemed unable to take advice, always quarreled with his superiors, demanded complete obedience and loyalty from his staff, but rationalized his own opposition to authority as responsive to a higher need.

Unfortunately, it is mostly the negative side of MacArthur's character that emerges in the *Reminiscences*. One is surprised that a man who was generally conceded even by his critics to have been brilliant, a genius, "packed with brains," could have written so poor a book. There is in it little sign of high intellect, of noble purpose, and of a grand vision of the future of mankind. The writing is undistinguished, pompous, and self-righteous in tone. There are long testimonials, some in the text, some in footnotes, from numberless public figures extending over half a century bearing witness to the greatness of his deeds—as though he needed such testimonials. Virtually every decoration and honor he received—and he was the most decorated soldier in American history—is noted.

The ego, the sensitivity to criticism, the conviction in his own rightness, the tendency to place himself in the center of affairs, to take credit for himself and place blame on others—all the traits that mar MacArthur's greatness are evident in the *Reminiscences*. He speaks of "my forces," "my plan," "my Alabama cotton-growers," "my Iowa farmers." He writes about his decisions and actions as though he were a sovereign unto himself. He pictures himself constantly beset by difficulties, the hostility of unnamed enemies, the stupidity of smaller men, and opposition from a government that has fallen under the influence of Communists. Alone and unaided he goes to Pearl Harbor, where the Navy has assembled a vast paraphernalia of plans, maps, and talent, to persuade the President that his strategy for returning to the Philippines is correct, the Navy's wrong. Similarly at Wake Island in October 1950 he faced alone the array of talent that the President brought with him, and conquered.

The almost paranoiac quality that marked MacArthur emerges clearly in this volume. It can be noted as early as 1932, when he personally led the troops against the Bonus Marchers, whom he regarded as tools of a communist conspiracy. His role then, he believed, made him a major target of the Communists, as did his advocacy of military preparations in the 'twenties and early 'thirties. This conviction was strengthened in the years that followed and emerges finally as a full-blown plot led by unnamed persons high in government in Washington, aided by the British. He is shocked by the order to take transports from him at Luzon to send supplies to Russia and sees in this evidence of communist influence in Washington. "The Communists," he writes, "had never ceased their violent attacks against me and with the liberal extremists joining them, the crescendo was rising." His candidacy for the Presidency in 1948, he believed, made retaliation against him only "a question of time," and his opposition to Soviet efforts to secure a voice in the Occupation led finally to his relief. "It took several years," he writes, "but their day finally came."

MacArthur's propensity for individual action, for challenging his superiors is evident here also. A lesser man would have been broken quickly, but MacArthur used the technique as a means for his own spectacular advancement. A major on the general staff in 1917, he wrote the single dissenting opinion on a troop study for World War I. When Secretary of War Newton D. Baker called him in, he boldly recommended the use of a National Guard division and before long was named chief of staff to the division and promoted to colonel. Undoubtedly, there was more to it than this, as there was to his version of how, single-handed, he frustrated the attempt to break up the Rainbow Division in France and use its elements as replacements for other units. As chief of staff, he opposed President Roosevelt on budget cuts, and, by his own account, used very hard words indeed to get the President to withdraw his program. More than once in World War II he used his special position with the Australian Prime Minister to secure more men and material for his theatre than the Joint Chiefs of Staff was willing to grant on the basis of military priorities. When he became Allied commander of the Occupation, he proved more difficult to control and in the Korean War virtually set his policies against those of his government. Yet he claims at the end that he does not understand why he was relieved by Truman.

The promise of additional light on some of the more controversial aspects of MacArthur's career is, unfortunately, not fulfilled in the *Reminiscences*. For those who have followed his career, the book holds few surprises. No new chapters of his life, personal or public, are revealed, few new incidents or encounters with the great and near-great. Even the anecdotes have been told time and again. Perhaps that is part of the MacArthur legend.

But if it adds little that is new, the *Reminiscences* omits much that is an essential part of the MacArthur story. Curiously, it contains only a single brief reference to his first marriage, even though it lasted nine years. The lady's name is not even mentioned! Protesting his own admiration for the Navy, MacArthur quotes a conversation in which General Marshall criticized the Navy and Admiral King. His own much stronger criticism of the Navy he withholds. One would scarcely be aware from this book that Admiral Nimitz played a major role in the defeat of Japan. For MacArthur, the Joint Chiefs of Staff as the directing agency of the war against Japan does not seem to exist. In the *Reminiscences,* it is MacArthur who makes all the plans, except those that go badly, and who, from time to time, advises Marshall, rather than the other way round. Though he quotes extensively letters of congratulations, citations, and similar material, he often fails to include—or quotes only small portions of—more important dispatches and communications.

Nor is he always entirely open with his reader. On several occasions he refers to the lack of a unified command in the Pacific and says that he sought vainly to persuade the Joint Chiefs to establish such a command. What he had in mind was his own elevation to this command, and he quotes with approval a letter from Senator Lister Hill to this effect. No one was more concerned about unity of command than General Marshall, but he knew, as did everyone else, that it would be impossible to establish a unified command without giving it to MacArthur, and the Navy would never accede to this. At various times General Marshall and General Arnold were proposed for the command, and one officer searching for a solution to the problem even suggested that MacArthur be made Ambassador to Russia to get him out of the Pacific.

General MacArthur had a strong sense of history, and frequently calls on history in support of his policies, using such phrases as "history clearly shows" and "history teaches." Yet he ignores and distorts much of the history of the events in which he was involved. His version of the events surrounding the Japanese surprise attack on Clark Field in the Philippines on December 8, 1941, does little justice to the labors of historians and settles none of the outstanding problems. He blames the United States for failing to provide him, when he was Military Adviser to the Philippine Commonwealth, with materials for defense of the Islands, but never mentions that there existed in the Philippines a large U.S. Army command (which he himself once commanded) that had the mission of defending the Islands from attack. He implies he had no knowledge of the Germany-first strategy adopted in 1941, although it is a matter of record that he received a copy of the plan embodying this concept. He charges Washington with "managed news," although his theatre was regarded by most correspondents as having stricter censorship rules than any other. He declares that Australian defense plans in 1942 were defeatist, that he was responsible for placing the defenses forward to Port Moresby, and that his relations with the Australian political and military authorities were excellent. The Australian official history denies all these assertions and claims that MacArthur deliberately avoided giving the Australians their proper place in the conduct of the war and the command of their troops.

There may be a particular value in having a MacArthur view of events, but it is a view that most historians would accept only with major reservations and qualifications. "Among President Truman's many weaknesses," writes MacArthur, quoting an unnamed source, "was his utter inability to discriminate between history and histrionics." This characterization would seem to fit the General better than the President. . . .

All his life MacArthur was the center of controversy. Even before his burial, while his body lay in state, the controversy was renewed by the publication of two interviews he had given some years before, charging Washington and the British with obstructing his plans in Korea. (These charges, incidentally, are quite consistent with the point of view expressed in his and Whitney's books.) The *Reminiscences*, far from stilling the controversies, will only add fresh fuel to the fire. Those who admired and revered him during his lifetime will find in it evidence to support the charges he made and the policies he advocated. Others will find in it confirmation of their worst fears. He was always his worst enemy, and his autobiography will add nothing to his reputation. He should be remembered by his deeds, not his words.

Bibliographical Note

MacArthur's correspondence was extensive, but the most important collections of his papers are at the MacArthur Memorial Bureau of Archives in Norfolk, Virginia; the Federal Records Center in Suitland, Maryland; and at the National Archives in Washington, D.C. Frank C. Waldrop, ed., *MacArthur on War: His Military Writings* (New York, 1942), and Vorin E. Whan, ed., *A Soldier Speaks: Public Papers and Speeches of General of the Army Douglas MacArthur* (New York, 1965) are useful compilations of his major speeches and writings. MacArthur's *Reminiscences* (New York, 1964), published shortly after the general's death, may be ghost-written in parts; nonetheless, despite its occasional errors and its strong partisan tone, it is an interesting and helpful source.

There have been many biographies of MacArthur—most of them popular accounts, replete with MacArthur myths and inaccuracies. The best of them, in addition to the works excerpted in this volume by Gunther, James, Rovere and Schlesinger, Whitney, and Willoughby and Chamberlain, are: John Hersey, *Men on Bataan* (New York, 1943); Frazier Hunt, *The Untold Story of Douglas MacArthur* (New York, 1954); Clark Lee and Richard Henschel, *Douglas MacArthur* (New York, 1952); and Gavin Long, *MacArthur as Military Commander* (London, 1969).

There have been numerous books and articles which discuss specific aspects of MacArthur's career. In addition to those excerpted in this volume, they include Henry Reilly, *Americans All: The Rainbow at War* (Columbus, 1936), and William A. Ganoe, *MacArthur Close-Up: Much Then and Some Now* (New York, 1962), which describe MacArthur's life in wartime France and at West Point. Walter W. Waters, with William C. White, *B. E. F.: The Whole Story of the Bonus Army* (New York, 1933), and John W. Killigrew, "The Army and the Bonus Incident," *Military Affairs,* XXVI (1962): 59–65 throw a revealing light on MacArthur's role as chief of staff. MacArthur's efforts in the Philippines and in World War II are analyzed in: Sidney L. Huff, with Joe A. Morris, *My Fifteen Years with General MacArthur* (New York, 1964); Louis Morton, "War Plan ORANGE: Evolution of a Strategy," *World Politics,* XI (1959): 22–50; Manuel Quezon, *The Good Fight* (New York, 1946); Carlos P. Romulo, *I Saw the Fall of the Philippines* (Garden City, 1942); Samuel E. Morison, *History of United States Naval Operations in World War II* (Boston, 1958); and Jonathan M. Wainwright, with Robert Considine, *General Wainwright's Story* (Garden City, 1946). Plans to secure the 1944 Republican Presidential nomination for MacArthur are detailed in Arthur H. Vandenberg, Jr., ed., *The Private Papers of Senator Vandenberg* (Boston, 1952), while MacArthur's subsequent activities in Japan are treated in: Robert E. Ward, "The Legacy of the Occupation," in Herbert Passin, ed., *The United States and Japan* (Englewood Cliffs, N.J., 1966); Justin Williams, "Completing Japan's Political Reorientation, 1947–1952: Crucial Phase of the Allied Occupation," *American Historical Review*, LXXIII (1968): 1454–69; Lawrence S. Wittner, "MacArthur and the Missionaries: God and Man in Occupied Japan," *Pacific Historical Review*, XL (1971): 77–98; and Kazuo Kawai, *Japan's American Interlude* (Chicago, 1960). MacArthur's participation in the Korean War has attracted considerable attention; three of the most penetrating accounts are: John W. Spanier, *Korea and the Fall of MacArthur* (New York, 1960); Harry S. Truman, *Memoirs* (2 vols., Garden City, 1956); and I. F. Stone, *The Hidden History of the Korean War* (New York, 1952). Norman Cousins, "Douglas MacArthur," *Saturday Review*, XLVII (May 2, 1964): 18–19, provides a surprisingly sympathetic assessment of MacArthur's career from the pacifist viewpoint.

Index